ORACLE GOD OF DEVOTIONAL

ISBN: 9781087956664 (Paperback)

Any references to historical events, real people, or real places are used fictitiously. Names, characters, and places are products of the author's imagination.

Front cover image by Mark for Zonazin.
Book design by Designer; Mark for Zonazin.

Printed by Ingramspark, Inc., in the United States of America.

First printing edition 2021.

Someone once said, "They that walk; walks with the multitude. They that runs runs with a few and they that fly, fly alone". And then somebody added, "If you want to be among the many, all you need is common sense; you don't have to think before you walk. If you're going to run with the few, you need advice, but you need instruction if you're going to fly. That is why those who teach pilots to fly are called flight instructors.

Are you ready to fly? Then be instructed!

Stevie Okauru, the Oracle of God.
Founder & Senior Pastor

ORACLE OF GOD INTERNATIONAL MINISTRIES INC.
An International Full Gospel and Deliverance Prayer Ministry

www.oraclemiracle.org

ORACLE OF GOD
Devotional

JULY - DEC 2021

© Stevie Okauru

ZONAZIN PRESS

NEW YORK   NEW DELHI   TORONTO   SIDNEY

July 1ˢᵗ

BLESSED IN PRAISING GOD!

"Let the peoples praise You, O God.... Then the earth shall yield her increase, and God shall bless us." **[Psalm 67:5-6]**

Praise recognizes attributes. It is the expression of one's appreciation of the integrity of the subject of praise. **[Psalm 47:7]** says, *"...sing ye praises with understanding."* Praise is not about an event, nor is it about what a person has done, what a person is doing, or is going to do and or can do. Praise recognizes the traits of the source of events, while thanksgiving is the appreciation of such events.

Praise brings God's deliverance upon the "Praiser"! In **[Acts 16:16-26],** Paul and Silas, on the night preceding their execution, Paul told Silas, *"We've fasted and prayed; we had vigils to no avail; let us now praise the Lord."* As they did, God steps in and breaks their chains. The gates of the prison fell apart, and their deliverance came at the eleventh hour!

PRAISE GOD NOW:

Father, I give You glory, honor, and adoration. You are worthy of all my praise; Glory be to Your name! I magnify Your holy Name. King of Kings and the Lord of Lords! The Ancient of days, the I Am that I Am. Blessed be Your Holy Name! Thank You, Father, in Jesus' Mighty Name, I worship. Amen!

July 2ⁿᵈ

DIVINE PATH

"You make known to me the path of life; you will fill me with joy in your presence, with eternal pleasures at your right hand." **[Psalm 16:11]**

Living in depression exempts you from the divine direction. You cannot attract God's presence for divine guidance in depression. If you cannot be happy, you can never attract God, and if you cannot attract God, He cannot direct you. If you want divine direction and fulfill a divine purpose, living in worship and excitement is necessary for life. A life of joy and worship is non-negotiable in your Christian walk **[Psalm 89:15]**.

God's presence is the sustainer of joy. **[Psalm 16:11]**. If you cannot be happy, you can never attract God, and if you cannot attract God, you are not qualified for His direction. An attack on joy is an attack on Divine guidance. It is an attack on the anointing because the oil is sustained by joy. The devil knows that everything is tied to your happiness, so he confronts you all the time with the spell of joylessness. **[Psalm 45:7]**

It is impossible to fly higher when you feel low. Feeling low is not compatible with flying high. If you are not joyful, you can never hear God, and if you cannot hear God, you cannot know His direction for your life. *Thus, I admonish you to connect to God's presence through worship. That will guarantee your access to Divine guidance in Jesus' Mighty Name. Amen!*

July 3rd

WORD OF THE ORACLE

*"**On the Lord's Day,** I was in the Spirit, and I heard behind me a loud voice like a trumpet."* **[Revelation 1:10 NIV]**

ON THE LORD'S DAY [GREEK] *KURIAKOS HEMERA*

The Greek term for *'On the Lord's Day'* is **"Kuriakos Hemera,"** as used in the above text-verse. Strong's Concordance #2960:

That is the only mention of the Lord's Day in the New Testament. That was most likely the first day of the week; a day Believers gathered to worship and celebrate the Lord's Supper **[1st Corinthians 11:20].** *"Therefore, when you come together in one place, it is not to eat the Lord's Supper."*

Because Jesus Christ rose from the dead on that day, the early Church father Ignatius seems to allude to "The Lord's Day," as does Irenaeus.

Do you celebrate The Lord's Day?

Prayer: *Lord! Give me the grace to always celebrate you in Jesus' Gracious Name. Amen!*

First Sunday in July

ONE YEAR BIBLE PLAN: Job 27-28/ Acts 13:26-52

SUNDAY SCHOOL

RECEIVING GOD'S GRACE!

A. RECEIVING GOD'S SAVING GRACE REQUIRES OBEDIENCE: [Hebrews 5:9; Philippians 2:8-12].

1. For Jesus is "The Author [or source] of salvation to all who believe and obey." – **[Hebrews 5:9]** *"It was after He had proved himself perfect in this experience that Jesus became the Giver of eternal salvation to all those who obey him."*

2. Freedom from sin comes when one is willing to believe from the heart and the trust and obey Him – **[Romans 6:15-18]**

3. Such obedience involves:

   a. Trusting in Jesus Christ as God's Son who died for our sins – **[John 3:16]**

   b. Confessing your faith before men – **[Romans 10:9-11]**

   c. Repenting of your sins – **[Acts 17:30 AMP]**

   d. All the above culminating with being buried with Christ in baptism for the remission of our sins – **[Mark 16:15-16 NIV, Acts 2:38 AMPC]**

Memory Verse: [Acts 22:16] *"And now why are you waiting? Arise and be baptized, and wash away your sins, calling on the name of the Lord."*

<u>Prayer:</u> *Holy Spirit imparts my spirit, soul, and body with Your saving grace in Jesus' Precious Name. Amen!*

July 5th

".... The Jews found out that Jesus was there and came, not only because of him but also to see Lazarus, whom he had raised from the dead." **[John 12:1-9 NIV]**

WIDELY CELEBRATED!

Lazarus was relatively unknown before his death and was referred to as a certain Bethany man in **[John 11:1]**. But after Jesus raised him from death, he became a celebrity. Some breakthroughs can change your statues forever for good. When that happens, people will begin to seek after you. Within 24 hours, Lazarus moved from a certain man to the cynosure of all eyes. *I prophesy you will be celebrated in Jesus' Name! I place the mark of favor upon you, and your miracle will distinguish and announce you in Jesus' Gracious Name. Amen!*
Do you desire this prophecy? If so, place your right hand on your head and declare thus: *Lord Jesus! You singled out Lazarus for a distinguished miracle; visit me today with a life-changing miracle and give me an inspiration that will change my world in Jesus' name.* As you pray this prayer, be expectant and prepare for a rare miracle. *As the Lord liveth, I decree, the spirit of excellence is released upon you now in Jesus' Name. Amen!*

Prayer: *My miracle will distinguish and announce me in Jesus' Name. Amen!*

TESTIMONY TUESDAY

"All flesh would perish together, and man would return to dust. "If you have understanding, hear this; Listen to the sound of my words:" **[Job 34:15-16]**

"I sought employment many years after my postgraduate studies. I was utterly frustrated out of chains of disappointments before I met the man of God at OGIM. He prophesied as he prayed for me; he said in seven days; I will be gainfully employed, and my prayer point will change to; 'Lord, which of these three jobs should I accept.' To my utmost surprise, within 48 hours, I had two job offers. The third offer came on the third day. Glory to God! I am gainfully employed now after many years! Brother X.

The above testimony is just one of the numerous tales of God's ability to open closes doors in the lives of those who look up to Him. If your story is that of disappointments? There is hope for you. God can change your sad story to glory. It does not matter how bleak your situation may be right now or appears to be. **[Isaiah 45:2]** says He will make your crook path straight, in **[Isaiah 43:18-19]** He said He would make a way where there seems to be no way. God is aware of your situation. That is why He made all these promises to you, and He is more than able to fulfill them. So, keep up the faith, maintain a positive mental attitude, put on a pleasant countenance, and be blessed.

Prayer: *Father! Make a better way for me!*

July 7th

DEEP DIGGING: **OBEDIENCE AND GRACE!**

Obedience has nothing to do with meriting grace: Salvation is by grace, and "not by works of righteousness which we have done" – **[Titus 3:4-5 AMP]**. It is solely by God's mercy and grace; we are saved "by the washing of regeneration and renewing of the Holy Spirit" – **[Titus 3:5]**. This phrase refers to the Holy Spirit's works, which instantly changes us by the cleansing of regeneration [which is the new birth], and this unique nature helps us live the Christian life. Renewing of the Holy Spirit is the continual process of Christian living enabled by the Holy Spirit, resulting in character and good works.

When a sinner trusts in Jesus Christ, he/she is baptized into Christ: We are united with Christ in baptism into His death and therefore rises to walk in newness of life **[Romans 6:3-8]**. Baptism expresses faith as words express an Idea. There can be an idea without words, but words and actions typically express ideas. Water baptism by immersion is a symbol of the spiritual realities of the union of Christ and believers. We are "clothed" with Christ to enjoy all the blessings made possible by Jesus Christ's death! **[Galatians 3:26-27 AMP/TLB; Hebrews 7:24-25 AMPC]**. Through "washing of regeneration and renewing of the Holy Spirit," one is truly "born again of water and the Spirit!" – **[Titus 3:5; John 3:5]**

CONCLUSION: God has ordained: *That through faith and repentance, with baptism into Christ, we might receive the extraordinary grace of God!*

Why don't more people respond to God's saving grace? They do not appreciate, nor do they understand the "need" for grace: They consider themselves good, moral people. Yet, in nearly every example of salvation in Acts, those saved were religious and very moral already! But as Isaiah said, *"All our righteousness's are as filthy rags"!* **[Isaiah 64:6]**

Many are still not aware of the "provision" of grace: They think that they are too sinful to receive God's grace: Yet God desires all to be saved and has provided Jesus Christ *"a ransom for all."* – **[1ˢᵗ Timothy 2:3-6 TLB]**

Many have not been taught the proper "reception" of grace: Many are told to *"Say the sinner's prayer"* without telling them what Jesus and His apostles commanded people to do to receive God's saving grace. People need to listen to Jesus Christ and His apostles, not modern opiniated preachers! **[Mark 16:15-16, Acts 2:36-38; Acts 22:16]**

We saw at the beginning of our study that Paul's ministry was: *"To testify to the gospel of the grace of God."* **[Acts 20:24]. So, in closing, let us add the words of Peter to that of Paul's commission:** *"Testifying that this is the true grace of God in which you stand."* **[1ˢᵗ Peter 5:12].**

How do you relate to God's grace? Have you received the grace of God? Are you standing in the pure grace of God?

July 8th

WEALTH OF GOD'S GRACE

"But by the grace of God I am what I am: and his grace which was bestowed upon me was not in vain; but I labored more abundantly than they all: yet not I but the grace of God which was with me." [**1st Corinthians 15:10**]

Grace is the reason Christ went to Calvary. Grace covers our errors and colors our efforts. God's grace is the distinguishing factor in people's lives. The difference between the two believers is the dimension of grace they access. There are diverse levels of grace. There is grace; there is a great grace; there is exceeding grace and multiplied grace. That is why we must grow in grace in [**2nd Peter 3:18**]. Your present level of grace can increase. The difference between Paul and the other apostles was grace. He said *by the grace of God, I am what I am*. It means, *'If you like my results, what you need is the level of grace in which I operate.'*

The acronym for G-R-A-C-E is God's Riches At Christ's Expense. God sacrificed Christ for His riches to be available to us. **[Romans 5:8; 2nd Corinthians 8:9].** Grace is God's seal of approval and acceptance. It covers our errors and colors our efforts. To access God's grace, live a humble life. **[James 4:6, 1st Peter 5:5, Proverbs 3:34].** And you activate God's grace at the prayer altar. So, ask God to grant you the spirit of humility.

Prayer: *Lord, Multiply your grace in my life!*

July 9th

"…. bound hand and foot with graveclothes: and his face was bound about with a napkin. Jesus saith unto them, lose him, and let him go." **[John 11:30-44]**

GARVE CLOTHES!

In **[verse 44 of John 11]**, *"…. Lose him and let him go."* is always overlooked. Consider this, say Lazarus was left with the grave clothes on as he got out of the grave. He would have been encumbered. At best, he would have been able to only hop from point A to point B like a Kangaroo. That is a graphic illustration of many believers' lives. They are incapable of recording any breakthrough whatsoever in life because of encumbrance in their life. When they were dead in sin, they had involved themselves in all sorts of demonic activities, such as occultism, idolatry, witchcraft, wizardry, charms, and talisman, that entangled and bound them. And now that their souls are saved and regenerated, they need some sort of deliverance from all the demonic deposits. Unless some exorcism is done to lose them, they remain bound in life just like Lazarus was, until he was loosed.

However, at the order of Jesus Christ, the grave clothes were removed, and total freedom and liberty came to Lazarus. *Today, as the Oracle of God, I command every hindrance to your freedom is now removed in Jesus' Mighty Name!*

Prayer: *I set ablaze every garment of death in my life!*

July 10th

WORD OF THE ORACLE

"He who has an ear, let him hear what the Spirit says to the churches. To him, who overcomes I will give to eat from __the tree of life,__ which is amid the Paradise of God."
[Revelation 2:7]

THE TREE OF LIFE [GREEK]: *XULON TES ZOES*
The Greek term for *'The Tree of Life'* is *"Xulon Tes Zoes,"* as used in the above text-verse and in **[Revelation 22:2 and Revelation 22:14]**. Strong's Concordance #2222, 3586:
The Greek term denotes *"A Tree that gives Life,"* means, eternal life **[John 20:31]**. This tree symbolizes the eternal life God has made available to humanity. The tree of life was present in the Garden of Eden, but its fruit was not eaten because Adam and Eve had fallen into sin. **[Genesis 2:9; Genesis 3:24]**.
Jesus came to restore humankind and to offer us again the tree of life **[Revelation 2:7]**. Those in the New Paradise, the New Jerusalem, will partake in the tree of life forever **[Revelation 22:2]**.
__Prayer:__ *Lord Jesus, you are the vine of life graft my life unto your life?*

Second Sunday in July

SUNDAY SCHOOL: **GRACE AND BELIEVERS PT 1/4**

Grace is a word that conveys excellent hope and comfort to the believer. It is a word that Paul loved to use. Every epistle that he wrote [except for Hebrews], begins and ends with a mention of this word, e.g., **[1st Thessalonians 1:1]** *"Paul, Silvanus, and Timothy, to the church of the Thessalonians in God the Father and the Lord Jesus Christ: Grace to you and peace from God our Father and the Lord Jesus Christ."*
What does this word mean? How is it used in the New Testament? What essential things should we keep in mind concerning "grace"? In this study, we shall focus on this beautiful word and how it relates to believers.

THE DEFINITION OF "GRACE"

1. **THAT WHICH GIVES JOY, PLEASURE, AND DELIGHT:** This is the original idea of the Greek word *"Charis,"* the root word for the English word charismatic.

   a. Grace is used in the N.T. about SPEECH; the words of Jesus were spoken with grace. **[Luke 4:22]**

   b. So, as Christians, Christ-followers, our word is to impart grace to our listeners. **[Ephesians 4:29; Colossians 4:6]**

2. **GOOD-WILL, LOVINGKINDNESS, AND FAVOR:** This way, grace is used: Of the

kindness of a master towards his servants and especially of God towards us.

a. **"CHARIS** *contains the idea of kindness bestows upon one who does not deserve it."* Grace is the means God uses to bestows favors even upon the ill-deserving. It grants sinners the pardon of their offenses and bids them to accept eternal salvation through Christ. **[Ephesians 2:5]**

b. This definition of grace prompts us to think of it most often as "unmerited favor."

3. **GRACE IS A SPIRITUAL STATE OR CONDITION IN WHICH ONE ENJOYS GOD'S FAVOR:** When we accept God's grace, we are in a "State of Grace" **[Romans 5:1-2; 1ˢᵗ Peter 5:12]**

4. **GRACE FUNCTIONS AS AN EXPRESSION OF GRATITUDE FOR FAVOR BESTOWED:**
[1ˢᵗ Timothy 1:12] *"Here in this text, grace connotes thanks as in the English word [I thank Jesus Christ.]* When we say let us share the grace, we are saying let us give thanks, even before and after a meal. And as we share the grace after every meeting.

Such are the main ways the word GRACE is used in the New Testament. *In connection with this word, there are certain things we should always keep in mind, and that will be the subject of our study next lesson by the grace of God.*

happy sunday

GRACE AND MONEY Part 1

"For ye know the grace of our Lord Jesus Christ, that, though he was rich, yet for your sakes, he became poor, that ye through his poverty might be rich." **[2nd Corinthians 8:9]**

Is God interested in financial provision for you? Ministries have been teaching prosperity for decades, with no tangible change. And some say it is because it is not the church's business to teach prosperity but morality. In the Old Testament, we see Godly people prosper, and their wealth was attributed to their relationship with God. For example, Abraham, Isaac, Jacob, Joseph, David, Solomon, etc.

After the resurrection of Christ, **[2nd Corinthians 9:8-9 NLT]** says God will always provide all our needs. It assures us that every need will be met. God is interested in our provisions. Your provision has been provided on the platform of grace. Whatever God has provided for your wellbeing was provided on the platform of grace. Freedom from the consequences of sin, including poverty, came on the platform of grace, not works. You can never work hard enough to receive freedom from evil nature. Hard work alone will not prosper you but the grace of God that supplies all your needs according to His riches. There is nothing you can do to be justified before God. Thus, God sent His only Son to die for us, a gift from God, and this gift includes money. Glory to God!

TESTIMONY TUESDAY

"…….. declares the LORD, I will do to you the very thing I heard you say" **[Numbers 14:28 NIV]**

POWER OF CONFESSION

"I want to let you know how highly lifted I am by your book 'The Oracle of God' Devotional. Especially the message on positive confessions."

I feel so alive when I read your book. I know about creative dispositions and positive confessions. However, your anointing brings a new level of results to it. I do not feel depressed anymore. And I can now testify to receiving positive confirmations of my confessions. Your book enthuses me. More grace, a great man of God indeed. Glory to God!

Brother XX.

You, too, can receive your own tremendous and mighty testimonies if only you believe and act on what you believe by just confessing them and possess what you confess.

<u>Prayer:</u> *Lord! Give me the grace to believe and receive what I confess from your word in the Name of Jesus Christ. Amen!*

DEEP DIGGING: **GRACE AND THE BELIEVER PT 2/4**

Let us dig deep into the absolute truth of scriptures:

1) HOW GRACE SAVES!
2) WHY GRACE NEEDS HOLINESS?
3) WHAT DOES IT TAKE TO LIVE HOLY?
4) WHY SHOULD WE GROW IN GRACE?
5) HOW TO GROW IN GRACE?
6) WHY SOME RECEIVE GOD'S GRACE IN VAIN:
7) HOW PEOPLE RECEIVE GOD'S GRACE IN VAIN!

Let us start with:

<u>A. GRACE SAVES US:</u> Salvation is first, foremost, and always a matter of grace! **[Ephesians 2:5-8]**

a. God does not owe us anything: What we deserve is eternal damnation because we are all sinners. **[Romans 3:23]**

b. Salvation is a gift: Which God in His lovingkindness offers to us all. **[Romans 6:23b; Titus 3:3-7 AMP]**

Eternal life or regeneration is used 42 times in the Old King James Version of the New Testament Bible, and it usually refers to something we receive as a gift at the time of belief in the gospel: **[John 3:16 TLB; John 5:24 AMPC; John 6:40].**

However, 11 out of the 42 times, eternal life is presented as something we attain, something that must be attained. **[Romans 6:22; Romans 2:7; Matthew 19:16; Matthew 19:29; Mark 10:17; Mark 10:30 AMPC; Luke 10:25 AMPC; Luke 18:18; John 12:25-26 AMP; Galatians 6:8]**

From these scriptures, it is safe to say that eternal life is not a static entity. Eternal life is a dynamic and growing relationship with Christ. **[John 10:10, John 17:3].** Through living in the obedience of faith, we can fully enjoy God's gift of eternal life.

2. No matter what God may call upon us to do is not enough to merit grace: To receive His grace, when we do those things, *such as repent, believe, confess Jesus Christ as Lord, and be baptized,* still in no way can we ever say that we earn or merit salvation. Even in serving Him, we are still unworthy servants. **[Luke 17:10 AMPC].**

So, no matter what God may call upon us to do: To receive His grace, when we do those things, *such as repent, believe, confess Jesus Christ as Lord, and be baptized,* still in no way can we ever say that we earn or merit salvation. Even in serving Him, we are still unworthy servants. **[Luke 17:10]**

3. Therefore, we must forever remember and never forget that only by God's grace is salvation possible!
NEXT WEEK WE WOULD CONTINUE BY THE GRACE OF GOD.

July 15th

GRACE AND YOUR FINANCE Part 2

"For ye know the grace of our Lord Jesus Christ, that, though he was rich, yet for your sakes, he became poor, that ye through his poverty might be rich." **[2nd Corinthians 8:9]**

Our financial blessing is on the platform of grace. What God has provided can only come on the platform of grace. **[2nd Corinthians 8:9 NLT]** Jesus went to the cross and took our place. In **[2nd Corinthians 5:21]**. Christ's death on the Cross was the substitution. He took our sinful nature so we can be freed. That is a gift of God. That is precisely how it works for our financial provisions. If you are a Christian and you label yourself poor, you lie. In God's record, there is no poverty you can claim. For Christians, life happens in two-folds: The spiritual and physical realm. We must get the spiritual right to rectify the physical. Your prosperity is provided on the platform of Grace.

[Romans 4:1-4]. If God has provided for you on the platform of grace and you begin to work for it, you are on a different channel. You do not struggle for God's given gift. You can only activate grace by faith. Believing God, even when your situation is contrary. **[Romans 4:16–17]** if you are to operate at that level of grace, you must know the God you believe in. He can make the impossible possible. He calls what is not into existence. If what He promises does not exist, He creates it.

July 16th

"………do as thou hast said, and do even so to Mordecai the Jew, that sitteth at the king's gate: let nothing fail of all that thou hast spoken". **[Esther 6:1-10]**

MY BOOK OF RECORD

[Esther 6:1-3] *"On that night could not the king sleep, and he commanded to bring the book of records of the chronicles….?*

For years, Mordecai's good deeds went unrewarded. He did his work diligently and faithfully without recognition. He even saved the life of the King by unveiling a Coup De Tat attempt. Yet, instead of promotion, Haman, the king's chamberlain, tried to destroy him. But one day, God remembered him and caused the king to lose his peace until he rewarded Mordecai.

Have your good works gone unsung and un-praised for years? Have you been persecuted for being upright and honest instead of being rewarded? Are you experiencing rejections, discrimination, and workplace wickedness? *I prophesy your days of despair are over because God has opened the book of remembrance for you this day in the Name of Jesus Christ.* So, be not despondent because when God opens, no one can shut. *Every door of affliction in your life is effectively shut now in the Name of Jesus.* The Lord has chosen to remember you, *so your life is about to change for the best in Jesus' Name. Amen!*

July 17th

WORD OF THE ORACLE

*"John, to the seven churches in the province of Asia: Grace and peace to you from him who is, and who was, and who is to come, and from the **seven spirits** before his throne."* **[Revelation 1:4]**

SEVEN SPIRITS [GREEK]: *HEPTA PNEUMATA*
The Greek term for 'Seven Spirits' is *"Hepta Pneumata"* as used in the above text-verse and in **[Revelation 3:1; Revelation 4:5 and Revelation 5:6].** Strong's Concordance #2033; 4151. This term connotes the "Sevenfold Spirit." The number seven represents completeness. This Divine Spirit's description depicts the Holy Spirit's sevenfold energy, perfect, complete, and universal energy. The term sevenfold probably corresponds to the earlier reference to the seven churches. The Spirit of God is One in His essence but numerous in His gracious influences.
This expression's origin could have been a simplified interpretation of **[Isaiah 11:1-2]** in the Greek Old Testament, which was taken to reference the sevenfold spiritual blessings.

Prayer: *Father, release your seven-fold Spirit upon my life in the Name of Jesus Christ.*

Third Sunday in July

SUNDAY SCHOOL: **GRACE AND BELIEVERS PT 3/4**

Today in part three of GRACE AND BELIEVERS: Let us dig deep into more scriptural truth like:

1) WHY GOD'S GRACE REQUIRES HOLY LIVING!
2) WHAT DOES IT TAKE TO LIVE HOLY?
3) WHY MUST WE GROW IN GRACE?
4) HOW CAN WE GROW IN GRACE?
5) WHY SOME RECEIVE GOD'S GRACE IN VAIN:
6) HOW CAN ONE RECEIVE GOD'S GRACE IN VAIN!

Let us start with why grace REQUIRES HOLINESS:

B. WHY GOD'S GRACE REQUIRES HOLY LIVING!

1. Some believers think since we are saved by grace, we are free to do whatever we like: Yet the "grace of God teaches us" to:
    a. Reject ungodliness and worldly lusts.
    b. Live soberly, righteously, and godly.
    c. And to look forward to the blessed hope and glorious appearance of Jesus Christ. **[Titus 2:11-13 AMP; TLB].**

3. The unmerited favor of God is no excuse to go on sinning! **[Romans 6:1-3 TLB; AMP].**

4. **In grace, Jesus gave Himself for us:** That He might redeem us from every lawless deed and thus purify

for Himself His special people, zealous for every good work – **[Titus 2:14]**.

C. WHAT DOES IT TAKE TO LIVE HOLY? *HOLY LIVING REQUIRES GOD'S GRACE!* To live "Soberly, righteously and godly" requires the grace of God: We cannot do it on our own, but with God's grace, with His help, and divine enablement, we can!

    a. He works in us to do His goodwill. [Philippians 2:12-13]. By His strength, we can do all the things He desires of us: **[Philippians 4:13 TLB]**

D. WE MUST STRIVE TO GROW IN GRACE!
1. That is especially true if we are going to live holy lives: Scriptures commands us to grow in grace – **[2nd Peter 3:18]**
2. It is not enough just to experience God's grace in forgiven sins: God has so much more to share with us, both in this age and the coming one – **[Ephesians 2:7 AMPC]**.
3. That explains Paul's greetings and benedictions. **[1st Thessalonians 1:1]**.

Memory Verse: [1st Thessalonians 5:28] *"The grace of our Lord Jesus Christ be with you. Amen."*
<u>Prayer:</u> *Lord, give the grace to value grace!*

July 19th

[2nd Timothy 4:18] *"And I was delivered out of the mouth of the lion. And the Lord shall deliver me from every evil work and will preserve me......."*

DELIVERED!

The trend of calamities that have befallen humanity in recent times is a source of concern for the informed. Man, orchestrated disasters, and natural disasters have laid siege on humankind. When it is not Hurricane Katrina, suicide bombings in the Middle East or a vast oil spill in the ocean, or Covid-19 pandemic when it is not a flood in the East, it will be plane crashes in the west, Asia, and Africa.

Humanity is at the highest level of risk in history. All these are works of the devil. But in all, God promises to deliver us. And He is more than willing and able to bring His Word to pass. If God said it, that settles it, and so believe it and receive it.

So, fear not, for you bear the mark of Christ, and nobody will ever trouble you again. You are covered with the Blood of sprinkling. The Blood will separate and exempt you from evil. Israel's children lived in the same land as the Egyptians, but whereas the Egyptians cried because of their calamities, Israel's children were delivered. *I prophesy God shall deliver you from every evil work in Jesus' Name. Amen!*

Prayer: *Calamity shall never again be my identity!*

TESTIMONY TUESDAY

"... ... Therefore, Saul removed him from him, and made him his captain over a thousand; and he went out and came..." **[1ˢᵗ Samuel 18: 1-12]**

GOD SHALL MAKE A WAY!

As far as the palace was concerned, no position was advertised. All the principal officers of Saul were in place. But because God desired to elevate David, a post was created. Such miracles still happen. The testimony below is a typical example:

"I had worked conscientiously in my former company in expectation of a desired promotion. But at the end of my thirteenth month probation period, I was fired instead of promoted. So, I applied for various vacancies to secure another job. But none yielded results until I participated in the monthly three-day OGIM marathon fasting and praying in July 2019.

During the fast, I applied for a position in an organization. After waiting for a long time, I call the man of God in Raleigh, who said I should go to the company to get the job. At his word, I went to the company and asked for an opportunity to work with them. To the glory of God, even though there was no more vacancy, they held a series of meetings to create a position for me. Today my new role is better than expected. God is great, Hallelujah!" Brother TJ.

Prayer: *Lord Miraculously create a place for me at the top!*

DEEP DIGGING: **GRACE AND THE BELIEVER: PT 4/4**
HOW CAN WE GROW IN GRACE?

We grow in grace through:

a. Heeding God's Word **[Acts 20:32 AMPC]**

b. Drawing near to God in prayer and worship **[Hebrews 4:16 TLB]**

c. BY LEARNING OF JESUS CHRIST: **[2ⁿᵈ Peter 3:18 and Matthew 11:29]**

SOME RECEIVE GOD'S GRACE IN VAIN: God's Word pleads with us not to receive God's grace in vain. **[2ⁿᵈ Corinthians 6:1].** So, it is possible to receive grace in vain!

HOW CAN ONE RECEIVE GOD'S GRACE IN VAIN!

a. We fall from grace or reject grace by seeking justification for sin elsewhere. **[Galatians 5:4]**

b. Apart from the reference to Moses's Law, if we seek to be justified by any salvation system by works alone, we will fall from grace!

c. We reject grace by using God's grace as an excuse for licentiousness – **[Jude 4 AMPC].** Some use grace as an excuse for shameless behavior, and yet God's grace requires holy living **[2ⁿᵈ Timothy 2:11-14 AMP]**

d. We receive grace in vain by willfully committing sin, thereby despising the Spirit of grace **[Heb. 10:26-31].**

For such a person, there remains no sacrifice of their sin. Only a fearful expectation of judgment. Because through such willful and impenitent sin one:

a. **Tramples on the Son of God.**
b. **One discounts the Blood of the covenant** [i.e., Jesus' Blood] by which we are sanctified [i.e., saved]
c. **We thus commonizes and trivializes Christ's sacrifice on the Cross of Calvary.**
d. **And it is an insult to the Spirit of Grace.**

CONCLUSION: What a terrible thing it would be to receive God's grace in vain! To have received God's grace at one point, but then make it all worthless.

And it is just as terrible: Not to receive grace all! Or having received it, and not to grow in it! We are encouraged, in the book of Hebrews, to: *"Look diligently lest anyone fall short of the grace of God." –* **[Hebrews 12:15].** So, *"...Let us have grace, by which we may serve God acceptably with reverence and godly fear." –* **[Hebrews 12:28; Hebrews 13:9; Hebrews 13:25].**

Have you received the extraordinary grace of God in your life? Then you must impart grace and spread the goods news of the gospel of God's grace to your world. And this is the topic of a new series we would start next week.

Prayer: *Lord grant me grace, by which I may serve you acceptably with reverence and godly fear."*

July 22nd

GRACE AND YOUR FINANCE Part 3

"For you know the grace of our Lord Jesus Christ, that though he was rich, yet for your sake, he became poor, so that you through his poverty might become rich." **[2nd Corinthians 8:9 NIV]**

In parts 1 and 2, we learned that God had made believers' provisions to enjoy through grace. Some seek to know if God's involvement is only limited to our spiritual lives. And it is also good to know that God is interested in our financial well-being base on the finished work of Jesus Christ on the Cross. Jesus paid for our sins and their consequences when He died on the Cross, and poverty is one of the results of sin.

God's provision is not received on the platform of efforts but by grace. It is a gift we access through God's empowerment. Once we are off the channel of grace, we are off divine provisions. **[Hebrew 4:3]** tells us that we have rest when we function at this level of faith. Believers' provision is created in the spirit realm. Breakthroughs are created first in the realm of the spirit and translated into physical reality. **[Revelation 13:8]** states that Christ's work on the cross was finished from the foundation of the earth. Thus, there is rest for believers. So, to access the fullness of God's blessings, we must enter God's rest. **[Hebrews 4:10]**.

Prayer: *Holy Spirit, help me rest in your grace!*

July 23rd

GRACE AND YOUR FINANCE Part 4

"For you know the grace of our Lord Jesus Christ, that though he was rich, yet for your sake, he became poor, so that you through his poverty might become rich." **[2nd Corinthians 8:9 NIV]**

[John 5:19-20] says the miracles Jesus did were already done spiritually. So, your financial miracle is spiritually done. But how do you bring them into reality? You act! You must take responsibility and do something in the physical for the spiritual reality to manifest. Grace can exist without results. **[1st Corinthians 15:10]**. Despite God's promise to Abraham and Sarah, they still had to meet as husband and wife to fulfill it.

Grace gives you the capacity to solve problems for others, thereby adding value to their lives. Money is only a means of exchange of values. You get money when values are exchanged for it. Grace gives you the capacity to add value to people's lives. **[Luke 4:18-19]**. When you solve problems, values go out of you, and value returns to you. The beginning of corruption is to want something valuable without offering value in exchange for it. Grace or the anointing gives you the capacity to add value to people's lives by solving problems. In **[Genesis 41:37-40]**, Joseph got to the palace because he solved problems.

So, at what level are you solving problems?

Prayer: *Lord, add value to my life I do to others!*

July 24th

WORD OF THE ORACLE

"I looked, and there before me was a pale horse! Its rider was named Death, and **Hades** *was following close behind him. They were given power over a fourth of the earth to kill by sword, famine, and plague, and by the wild beasts of the earth."* **[Revelation 6:8]**

HADES [GREEK]: *HADES*

The Greek term for 'Hades' is *"Hades"* as used in the above text-verse and in **[Revelation 20:13-14; Luke 16:23; Acts 2:27, Acts 2:31]**. Strong's Concordance #86: The Greek word means *"the place of the unseen."* It designates the invisible world of the dead, as does the Hebrew word *"Sheol."*

All people who die go to Hades because all the dead passes from the visible world to the invisible. The association between Death and Hades is, therefore, a natural one. Unfortunately, this word has often been associated with hell, a place of eternal punishment. But there is a different Greek word for hell; it is *'Gehenna'* **[Mark 9:43-45].**

We cannot avoid Hades, but we can avoid hell by believing in Jesus Christ and receive eternal life.

Prayer: *Lord, help my faith and save me from hell!*

Fourth Sunday in July

SUNDAY SCHOOL: **THE GREAT COMMISSION ACCORDING TO MATTHEW**
NATURE OF DISCIPLESHIP [Matthew 28:18-20 AMPC]

1. **In Matthew's account of** "The Great Commission,"the main idea of Jesus' command is:
    a. "Go make disciples of all nations" **[Matthew 28:18-20]**
    b. Jesus wanted His apostles to make disciples: But you must be a disciple to make disciples. You cannot give what you do not have. **[Acts 3:6]**

2. Are you a disciple of Jesus?
    a. You may believe in Jesus Christ.
    b. You may even attend church regularly.
    c. But is that what it means to be His disciple?

1. **THE DEFINITION OF A DISCIPLE:** The word "Disciple" literally means a learner. "A disciple is one who accepts and assists in spreading the doctrines of a mentor: A disciple is a convinced adherent of a school of thoughts and the idealism of an individual's teachings and doctrines."

    a. It denotes "one who follows another's teaching."
    b. A disciple was not only a learner but also an adherent.

c.   Disciples are imitators of their teachers.

2.   **What are the goals of being a disciple?**

   a.   **As stated by Jesus:** As a disciple, your goal is to be like your teacher: **[Luke 6:40]** *"A disciple is not above his teacher, but everyone who is perfectly trained will be like his teacher."*

   b.   **To be His disciple,** then, is to strive to be like Him, to be like God. **[Ephesians 5:1-2 AMPC]** *"Therefore be imitators of God [copy Him and follow His example], as well-beloved children [imitate their father]. And walk-in love, [esteeming and delighting in one another] as Christ loved us and gave Himself up for us, a slain offering and sacrifice to God...."*

   c.   **You become like God** when you strive to be like your teacher; that is, if your teacher strives to be like Jesus! **[1ˢᵗ Corinthians. 11:1-2 AMPC; 1ˢᵗ Corinthians 4:16; Philippians 3:17]**

   - *CHRIST SUFFERING BROUGHT THE GOSPEL.*
   - *THE APOSTLE SUFFERED TO MAKE IT AVAILABLE.*
   - *SO, WE MUST RECEIVE IT WITH JOY DESPITE. GREAT SUFFERINGS.*

3. **Striving to be Christ-like is God's goal in redemption**: That we conform to the image of His Son. **[Romans 8:29].**
    Do you have a strong desire to follow Jesus and become like Him? Unless you do, you cannot indeed be His disciple.

Memory Verse: [1ˢᵗ Corinthians 4:16]*; "Therefore, I urge you, imitate me."*

July 26th

SPIRITUALLY HEAR AND SEE!

"Do you have eyes but fail to see, and ears but fail to hear? And don't you remember?" **[Mark 8:18 NIV]**

When Jesus walked the earth, multitudes heard Him speak. Many; saw and heard Him. But Jesus said to His disciples, the twelve Apostles, He said, the people do not see, even though they have eyes. They do not hear, even though they are not deaf. But you are blessed because you can see and hear.

My question is: Are you blessed by what you see and hear? If you are receptive to everything the Lord seeks to convey to you, you are blessed. And it is possible to be in God's kingdom with eyes and ears that God opens to His freshness, His new and creative ways in a new world system today. With spiritually opened eyes, you see things that others do not see. You hear things others cannot hear; you discern things others cannot understand. You will be moving with the kingdom in motion.

God's kingdom is now manifest in an impressive dimension in this dispensation globally. *My prayer is that you will not only hear and see but also partake in the great move of the Spirit of God this season in the Name of Jesus. Amen!*

Prayer: *Lord, open my ears and eyes to hear and see the inaudible and the invisible in Jesus' Name. Amen!*

TESTIMONY TUESDAY

One Year Bible Plan: Psalm 49-51/ Acts 28:16-31
"Behold, I am the Lord, the God of all flesh; is there anything too hard for Me?" **[Jeremiah 32:27 AMPC]**

NOT TOO HARD FOR GOD

There is this testimony in one of our meetings. It was about a man whose left kidney was removed in surgery. The doctors spent hours operating on him. But then, in our revival, The Great Physician, Jehovah Rapha, sent His Healing Word, and the Word of God came by the Oracle: *"... There is someone here, one of your kidneys has been removed, and the second one is troubling you, and God says I am giving you two new kidneys."* And the man said, whoa! So, God can choose me for healing in this crowd. That was a weekend in August 2019. On Monday, he went to the doctor, and the doctor examined him and said, *"What? I know what we went through when we did surgery on one of your kidneys, but there are two new ones!"*

When we talk about total recovery, we are talking about 'The One' who can make anything possible. In **[Genesis 18:9-14]**, God told Sarah she would have a son. Sarah was ninety years old, and her husband a hundred. It was a long time since she had her period. She laughed, and God said, why did you laugh? And God said, is anything too hard for me? You may have lost hope entirely concerning your expectations. But God is restoring unto you that which you have lost this season!

<u>Prayer:</u> *Lord! Do the impossible in my life today!*

WEDNESDAY, July 28th

DEEP DIGGING: **MARK TRUE DISCIPLES?**
1. One who abides in the words of Jesus – [John 8:31]
"Then Jesus said to those Jews who believed Him, "If you abide in My Word, you are My disciples indeed."
MARY ABIDING AT JESUS' TOMB: [John 20:10-12]. JESUS TAKING TO THE TEMPLE: [Luke 2:22-40]

> a. Abiding means being a diligent student of Jesus Christ.
> b. Abiding requires us to be doers of the Word; not just hears- **[Matthew 7:21-27 AMP]**

THE BLESSING OF DISCIPLESHIP IS IN THE DOING AND NOT JUST HEARING: [James 1:22-25 TLB; Joshua 1:8; Isaiah 1:19 TLB]. Obedience is willingly allowing God to be God in your life! You let go and let God!

2. A disciple is one who loves believers – [John 13:34-35] With love patterned after the love of Jesus, *"As I have loved you."* With a visible love. *"by this, all will know."*

GOD'S KIND OF LOVE:

[John 3:16] For God so loved the world that He gave His only begotten son. Because God loves us, note that God does not just love, God is love! **[1st John 4:16; 1st John 4:8; 1st John 4:19]**.

God does not just love; He is love. He is the real stuff, so because He is love, He does whatever He says. Love

never fails. Love covers a multitude of sin, a variety of faults, a multitude of wrongs, love never die, and God is love, so God never fails. **[1ˢᵗ Peter 4:8; 1ˢᵗ Corinthians 13:4-8 NIV]**
This level of love is only possible when we are born again – [1ˢᵗ Peter 1:22-23 TLB]

3. One who bears much fruit
   – [John 15:8 AMPC] *"My Father is glorified and honored by this when you bear much fruit and prove yourselves to be My [true] disciples."*
   a. Notice the word "much" also found in **[John 15:5]** *"I am the vine; you are the branches. He who abides in Me, and I in him, bears much fruit; for without Me, you can do nothing."*
   b. Jesus is not talking about an occasional good deed, but a lifestyle that prompts people to glorify God! **[Matthew 5:16; Hebrews 13:15 NKJV]**

In conclusion, to be a disciple of Jesus means more than just a casual church member; it requires: A commitment to the teachings of Christ, loving the brethren, and bearing fruit.
Now that we understand the nature of discipleship, how does one begin to be a genuine disciple?
For this answer, next week, we would return to our working Scripture **[Matthew 28:19-20].**

<u>Prayer:</u> *Lord! Give me the grace to love like You!*

July 29th

"……… it shall come unto him. He that trusteth in his riches shall fall, but the righteous shall flourish as a branch". **[Proverbs 11:24-28]**

FLOURISH UNHINDERD!

In his magnum opus, "The meaning of Service," Harry Emerson Fosdick wrote: *The Sea of Galilee and the Dead Sea are from the same source. It flows down, cool and clear, from the heights of Hermon and the roots of the cedars of Lebanon.*

The Sea of Galilee makes the beauty of itself because it has an outlet. It receives to release. It gathers its wealth and pours them out to fertilize the Jordan plain. But the Dead Sea with the same water source produces horror because it has no outlet. It gets to keep. Emerson's hypothesis maybe philosophy, but it is consistent with the Biblical truth of prosperity.

Do you desire to prosper? Learn to give. The Sea of Galilee and the Dead Sea are not fairy tales; they exist in the world today. God is interested in increasing humanity. When you get from God and release to others, you make yourself a channel of blessings. Consequently, you become blessed abundantly. Learn to give, learn to release God's gifts upon others, and you shall flourish unhindered in Jesus' Name. Amen!

Prayer: *Lord! Give the grace to give bountifully!*

GRACE AND YOUR FINANCE Part 4

"For you know the grace of our Lord Jesus Christ, that though he was rich, yet for your sake, he became poor, so that you through his poverty might become rich." **[2nd Corinthians 8:9 NIV]**

God has made provision for our enjoyment through grace based on the finished work of Christ. When we accept God through Christ, our spiritual reality changes and the nature of sin is removed. And it is on this platform, we are guaranteed prosperity.

Grace is receiving something you can never work for or deserve. Financial success for a Christian is a gift. You are rich because Jesus took your poverty in exchange for His riches.

Another way for the exchange of value is GIVING. That also follows the principle that *'If value leaves you, higher value returns to you.'*

In **[Luke 8:1-3],** Jesus added value to people's lives through healing and casting out demons from them. In return, value flowed back to Him in that they provided for His material needs. *I pray that God will give you the grace to add value to people's lives from henceforth in the Mighty Name of Jesus!*

Prayer: *Lord! Empower me to add value to people's lives!*

July 31st

WORD OF THE ORACLE

[Revelation 4:8] *"Each of the four living creatures had six wings and was covered with eyes all around, even under its wings. Day and night, they never stop saying: "'Holy, holy, holy is the LORD God **Almighty,'** who was, and is, and is to come."*

ALMIGHTY [GREEK]: *PANTOKRATOR*

The Greek term for 'Almighty' is *"Pantokrator"* as used in the above text-verse and in **[Revelation 11:17; Revelation 15:3; Revelation 16:7, Revelation 16:14].** Strong's Concordance #3841:

The Greek term means "One who has power over everything," in other words, the One in total control. God commands all the host of powers in heaven and earth, and He can overcome all His foes.

The title 'Almighty' often occurs in Revelation as this book unveils God's excellent control over all the universe throughout all history.

Prayer: *Almighty Jehovah do mighty things in my life today in the Mighty Name of Jesus Christ.*

First Sunday in August

SUNDAY SCHOOL: **HEAVEN'S WORTH**

As we go through this lesson, keep these thoughts in mind: *#1. Faithful Christians must often make many sacrifices—#2. There is a glorious reward in heaven and on earth here; that comes to those who remain faithful. #3. And the rewards will surely be worth whatever it cost:* **[Rom. 8:18; 2nd Cor. 4:17]**

But the question is, will heaven be worth it all? And the answer is a bold Yes! But it never hurts to be reminded of the cost and rewards of discipleship. So, what are **THE COST OF DISCIPLESHIP?**

IN EVERYTHING JESUS MUST COME FIRST:
   a.   Before one's self – **[Luke 9:23-24 AMPC]**
   b.   Before anyone else, including family – **[Luke 14:26; Matthew 10:34-37 AMPC]**
   c.   Before anything, the world **[Luke 9:25; Luke 14:33]**

WE MUST BE WILLING TO SUFFER FOR CHRIST:
   a.   We must be willing to bear our cross – **[Luke 14:27** Living in this ungodly world, following Jesus Christ will sometimes bring ridicule and persecution **[2nd Timothy 3:12 AMPC]**
   b.   The persecution may be physical – **[1st Peter 4:12-13]**
   c.   The persecution may be verbal – **[Luke 6:27-28]**

Other things we must endure for Christ's sake include:

    d. Personal weaknesses in our struggle against sin – **[1ˢᵗ Corinthians 9:27 AMPC]**

    e. Disappointments brought on by failing brethren – **[2ⁿᵈ Corinthians 11:29 AMPC]**

    1) E.g., whose apathy and neglect produce slothful service.

    2) E.g., whose irregular attendance makes it difficult to depend on them.

    3) E.g., whose unwillingness to serve creates extra burdens on those who do help.

    4) E.g., whose murmuring hinders the efforts of those who try to do something.

Even if we are blessed to escape such things, we must still be willing to expend time and effort in promoting the cause of Jesus Christ positively. Sometimes alone, or with few to help. Sometimes in difficult times and places, where few appreciate your efforts.

Discipleship can be costly. And we are often "hindered" and "burdened," with "trials, toils and "many a heartache." But the Lord tells us through His Word that *"Heaven Will Surely Be Worth It All."*

We shall continue in our next study!

<u>**Prayer:**</u> *Father, give the grace and wisdom to be a true disciple in the Name of Jesus Christ.*

August 2nd

GOD WILL MAKE YOU GREAT!

"My heart is fixed, O God, my heart is fixed: I will sing and give praise." **[Psalm 57:7]**

A long time ago, a young man was hated by his brothers, ignored by his parents, with no hope in the world ever to become great. But one day, despite everything he was going through, he said, *"My heart is fixed within me, I will praise God!"* And God answered and said, *"Son, my heart is also fixed within me, I will make you exceedingly great."* That man was David, today like David, you can say, my heart is fixed within me, I will praise the Lord. And God is going to reply, saying my heart is also set, to make you exceedingly great.

PRAISE GOD NOW!

Lord, my heart is fixed within me! I will praise you! I will magnify Your Holy Name! I will adore You all the days of my life! I will do Your Will! I will adore You! It does not matter what is happening to me; my heart is fixed. I will praise You! I will love You! I will lift You high daily in Jesus' Name!

BIRTHDAY PRAYERS: Lord, thank you for your children born this month. They are children of a new beginning, begin a new thing in their lives, bless and prosper them anew; let it be well with them, as they serve you in Jesus' Name. Amen!

TESTIMONY TUESDAY

"…. He hath put a new song in my mouth, even praise unto our God…." **[Psalm 40:3]**

CRIES TO SMILES!

"I came back from Nigeria to the US early last year with two 40 ft containers. However, I could not clear the container from the port due to customs duties and all sorts of regulations. After incurring unbelievable demurrage and charges, I could only get one of the containers out. Then the God of the Oracle intervened. My wife and I called the man of God. On narrating our ordeal, he placed us on a seven-day fast with some scriptures to use, and he declared; on or before the end of the fast, the container will be released. Even though I said Amen, I did not believe it was possible because of what I had gone through. But to my greatest and pleasant surprise, on the third day of the fast, the container was released with a letter of apology because the authority had overcharged my containers, and as a result, they are sending me a refund of $3,700.59 for compensations. Glory to God"! Brother James Adamu.

Saint, are you stuck in some financial spiderweb? *I prophesy the Lord is taking you out of your struggles now, and He is turning your cries to smiles in Jesus' Name. Amen!*

Prayer: *Father, turn my cries to smiles in Jesus' Name. Amen!*

DEEP DIGGING: **DISCIPLE'S REWARD**
REWARDS OF FAITHFUL DISCIPLESHIP

[2nd Corinthians 11:23-28 AMP] *"For we know that if the earthly tent [our physical body] which is our house is torn down [through death], we have a building from God, a house not made with hands, eternal in the heavens......"*

1. Anyone who endure much hardship and can look forward to:

    a. A house not made with hands **[2nd Corinthians 5:1]**

    b. The riches of God's grace **[Ephesians 2:7 AMPC]**

    c. A glorious transformation **[Philippians 3:20-21 AMPC]**

    d. A crown of righteousness **[2nd Timothy 4:8 AMPC]**

    e. A heavenly kingdom **[2nd Timothy 4:18]**

REWARD OF FAITHFUL DISCIPLESHIP?
[1st Corinthians 4:9-13]

If you suffer hardship in Christ, you can look forward to:

    a. An inheritance imperishable, undefiled, reserved in heaven: **[1st Peter 1:3-4 TLB]**

    b. A new heaven and a new earth, in which righteousness dwells: **[2nd Peter 3:13-14 TLB; Revelation 1:9]**

If you suffer tribulation and exile, you shall be blessed with:

a. The bliss of those who were triumphant over tribulation. **[Revelation 7:9-10; Revelation 7:13-17]**

b. The destiny of the redeemed, forever with God **[Revelation 21:1-7; Revelation 21:10-11; Revelation 21:22-27 *and* Revelation 22:1-5]**
IN CONCLUSION: *Can there be any comparison...?* Between a few years of service, even with hardship? And an eternity of bliss in the presence of God? We have learned from the words and lives of Paul, Peter, and John.
What if they could return and speak to us today?
What if our loved ones who died in Christ could return and speak to us today?
Would they not tell us?
"Heaven Will Surely Be Worth It All"?
Whatever the cost of following Jesus Christ in this life may be, may the words of this lesson and the promises of Holy Scripture remind and comfort us to be faithful and persevere in all we do in Jesus' Name. Amen!

Prayer: *Holy Spirit strengthens me in the time of hardship in the Name of Jesus Christ. Amen!*

<h1 style="text-align:center">August 5th</h1>

GRACE AND YOUR FINANCE Part 5

"For you know the grace of our Lord Jesus Christ, that though he was rich, yet for your sake, he became poor, so that you through his poverty might become rich." **[2nd Corinthians 8:9 NIV]**

In **[2nd Corinthians 9:6-10 NLT]**, we observe that giving aligns with the law of money. To give and be given, we must be working, and providing value for others.

[Ephesians 4:28] shows the complete cycle, where you see the two levels for provision in display. The first one is by adding value through work. The grace of God rests upon our resources generated from honest work, devoid of stealing or begging. Then there is the next level where you must give. What you give determines what you get. Giving must be done willingly and abundantly. When you begrudge giving value, it is proof that you are not expecting to receive value in return.

Know that whatever it is you have, you got it on the platform of grace. It was a gift given to you in the realm of the spirit before you got it physically. If you got it as a gift, you must be willing to show grace to others as well. You must let the cycle continue. Practice grace. Give some of what you have received. In **[Proverbs 11:24-25 NIV]**, we are motivated to demonstrate grace by being children of God. **[See Romans 8:32, Acts 4:32].**

August 6th

PERFORMED PROMISES!

"... .... favored and to be envied is she who believed that there would be a fulfillment of the things that were spoken to her from the Lord." **[Luke 1:45 AMPC]**

God does not speak empty words. What He says He does. He is not a man that He should lie: Nonetheless, the onus is on us to receive God's promises by praying through in faith.

Many delay God's promises unnecessarily by unbelief. Unbelief weakens God's hand. **[Matthew 13:54-58]** records that Jesus could not perform many miracles in Nazareth, not because Jesus had lost the power to perform miracles or that the demons were too difficult for Jesus to cast out. No! Jesus declared the words, but because the people did not believe Him, the word did not work for them. That is why **[Luke 1:45]** says, *"Blessed is she that believed..."*

Has God promised you anything through dreams and visions? Have His servants declared His Word over your life? Have you caught a Rhema in God's Word? Beloved, believe in the Lord and the power of His might, and He shall perform those things He promised in Jesus' Name. Amen!

Prayer: *Oh, God! I believe that you can **[Affix the promise]**; fulfill these promises for me in Jesus' Name. Amen!*

August 7th

WORD OF THE ORACLE

[Revelation 2:10] *"Do not fear any of those things which you are about to suffer. Indeed, the __devil__ is about to throw some of you into prison, that you may be tested, and you will have tribulation ten days. Be faithful until death, and I will give you the crown of life."*

DEVIL; SATAN [GREEK]: *DIABOLOS*

The Greek term for 'Devil' is ***"Diabolos"*** as used in the above text-verse and in **[Revelation 12:9; Revelation 12:12; Revelation 20:2; Revelation 20:10; Matthew 4:1; Acts 10:38].** Strong's Concordance #1228:

The Greek word for 'Satan' is "Satanas" **[Revelation 20:2; Revelation 20:7; Matthew 4:10; Romans 16:20]** Strong Concordance #4567: The word Diabolos signifies a slanderer, one who accuses another. Hence, another name was given to him: *"The accuser of the brethren"* **[Revelation 12:10].**

Satan's name signifies an adversary, one who lies in wait for or sets himself in opposition to another. These and other fallen spirit names point to different features of his evil character and deceitful operations.

Prayer: *Fire of God destroy the accusing finger of the enemy over my life in the Name of Jesus Christ. Amen!*

Second Sunday in August

SUNDAY SCHOOL: **ARE YOU A DISCIPLE OF JESUS? Part 1 of 4**

INTRODUCTION: In 'the Great Commission, notice Jesus' command in – **[Matthew 28:18-20]** *"Go therefore and make disciples of all the nations..."*

To "Make disciples" is the GOAL of evangelizing the world for Jesus Christ. *The question is: Are you a disciple of Jesus...?*

Perhaps you believe in Jesus Christ. You might even attend church services regularly. But is that what it means to be His disciple? *This study aims to make clear what is involved in being a true disciple of Jesus Christ. Let us start with:*

I.   THE DEFINITION OF DISCIPLESHIP

THE WORD DISCIPLE: Means a learner. It denotes one who follows another's teaching. A disciple is not just a learner but also an adherent of what they learn. For this reason, disciples were spoken of as imitators of their mentors.

THE GOAL OF A DISCIPLE: Stated by Jesus himself: It is to be like his/her teacher – **[Luke 6:40].** To be Christ's disciple, then, is to strive to be like Him! Which coincides with God's goal in the redemption of humanity **[Romans 8:29].**

Are you striving to follow Jesus and become like Him? Unless you do, it cannot be said that you are His disciple! Jesus gave us some identifying marks to help us identify a true disciple.

II. THE MARKS OF DISCIPLESHIP

1. ABIDES IN JESUS' WORDS: Jesus said to those who believed in Him must abide in His Word **[John 8:31]**. Just being a diligent student of the teachings of Christ does not make one a true disciple. It also requires one to be a "doer" of the Word – **[Matthew 7:21-27; James 1:22-25]**

2. LOVES THE BRETHREN: Consider what Jesus said to His followers in **[John 13:34-35]**. With love patterned after the love of Jesus *["As I have loved you"]*. With a love that is visible to the world *["By this, all will know"]*.

3. BEARS MUCH FRUIT: Jesus told His disciples in **[Jhon 15:8]**. Notice the word "much" **[In John 15:5]**. Jesus is not talking about an occasional good deed. But a lifestyle that prompts people to glorify God! **[Matthew 5:16; 1ˢᵗ Peter 2:12]**. Failure to bear much fruit will result in being severed from Christ. **[John 15:1-2]**. To be a disciple of Jesus Christ means more than just a casual church member. It requires commitment, especially regarding: **1) The teachings of Christ, 2) The love of the brethren, and 3) Bearing fruit.**

The commitment involved is apparent in our next lesson.

August 9th

BE RECONCILED TO GOD

"Now all things are of God, who has reconciled us to Himself through Jesus Christ, and has given us the ministry of reconciliation." **[2nd Corinthians 5:18]**

[Ezekiel 36:33-38] addresses the pre-condition for divine restoration. Upon restoration, Israel would become like the Garden of Eden, fertile, fruitful, and urbanized. Above all, God would once again hear and answer their prayers and would be glorified again by all, including the surrounding nations.

Note that God does the cleansing and restoration of the lost glory based on grace and for His Name's sake. That points to the New Covenant and the Holy Spirit's work based on the finished work of Christ on the Cross of Calvary.

Today, with the redemptive work completed, God works in us from the inside, where the Holy Spirit does the job of transformation **[Philippians 2:13]**. Our ruined lives now can be regenerated. We can be refreshed, re-occupied, or occupied by a New Holy Master **[2nd Corinthians 5:17-18]**. Thus, we must respond to God by being reconciled to Him.

<u>Prayer:</u> *Lord, hear my prayers for Your divine restoration and blessings in the Name of Jesus Christ.*

TESTIMONY TUESDAY

END OF REPROACH

"...... Daughter be of good comfort; thy faith hath made thee whole. And the woman was made whole from that hour". **[Matthew 9:20-22]**

"Excitement took the better of me when, in 1990, I was admitted to study medicine at the University of Ife in Nigeria. I quickly made new friends who introduced me to drinking; gradually, I became an alcoholic. It was so terrible that I could no longer do without alcohol. Over three decades later, I am a successful medical practitioner. But I was not happy. Because the addiction ensured I did not live a fulfilled life. I became a reproach as I was now known as a drunk. People do not want to deal with me because I was considered a low life. As such, I lost great opportunities. As a medical doctor, I tried everything in the book to no avail. In October last year, I came to the OGIM, and the man of God prayed for me, and the habit became history. Glory be to God!"
Dr. Walter Wilson.

The doctor was delivered of alcoholism by the power of God. Is any addiction, ailment binding you? Is joblessness, bareness, poverty, or repeated failure your issue? *Whatever it may be, I declare by the same anointing that break the yoke, the reproach in your life is broken now in Jesus' Mighty Name. Amen!*

WEDNESDAY, August 11th

DEEP DIGGING: **ARE YOU A DISCIPLE? Part 2 of 4**
THE COST OF DISCIPLESHIP

#1. JESUS MUST COME FIRST: This is made strikingly clear by Jesus Himself in **[Luke 14:25-26]**. Before anyone else, including members of your own family – **[Matthew10:34-37]**. Even before one's self – **[Luke 9:23-25]**.

#2. WILLING TO SUFFER FOR JESUS: We must take up our cross and follow Him **[Luke 14:27]**. To live a godly life in an ungodly world, we may find that following Christ sometimes involves ridicule and persecution **[2nd Timothy 3:12]**. Even if we are blessed to escape such things, we must still be willing to expend time and energy in promoting the cause of Christ.

#3. FORSAKING ALL TO FOLLOW JESUS: We must be ready to count the cost and bear what we lost in following Christ **[Luke 14:28-33]**. In other words, Jesus must be the King and Lord of our lives. Nothing can take precedent over Him and His will for us.

This cost and of discipleship required by Jesus caused many to turn from following Him. But Jesus was not trying to attract large crowds; He wanted disciples!

Is the cost worth it? I believe so. And we shall see this in our next lesson.

August 12th

KNOW HIM!

"That I may know him, and the power of his resurrection, and the fellowship of his sufferings, being made conformable unto his death." – **[Philippians 3:10]**

Ignorance kills! But not knowing God is even more lethal. **[Daniel 4:33].** Pharaoh was reluctant to free the Israelites because he was ignorant of God's power **[Exodus 5:2],** yet that was not enough to excuse him and his kingdom from God's judgment. God will not accept ignorance as an excuse for disobedience.

Knowledge empowers, and the knowledge of the Almighty is the ultimate empowerment. But how do we know God to draw maximum benefits from Him? How do we avoid walking contrary to His will? God is the source of all blessings. To know Him, you must first know Jesus. **[Matthew 11:27].**

Knowing Jesus Christ is understanding the mind of God, and those who know their God shall be strong and shall do exploits **[Daniel 11:32].** No wonder Paul prayed passionately to know Jesus intimately **[Philippians 3:10].** When we look at Paul's prayer, we may understand why he did great exploits in ministry. To achieve the same result, we also must be knowledgeable in God's Word. Search the Scripture daily to know Jesus Christ more **[John 5:39].**

August 13th

"As a cage is full of birds, so their houses are full of deceit......" **[Jeremiah 5:27]**

SPIRITUAL CAGE!

A cage is a structure of bars or wires to confine birds or other animals. Unfortunately, just as there are cages in the natural realm, there are invisible spiritual cells constraining human captives. The frightening part about **[Jeremiah 5:25-27]** is that God said this wickedness is done by "His" people, believers. That means even in God's Kingdom, there are vessels of dishonor that do wicked things, even unto fellow believers. **[Matthew 7:21-23]** says, *"Not every one that saith unto me, Lord, Lord, shall enter into the kingdom of heaven...."*

Many things can be in confinement in a person's life? A person's finances, health, and marriage can all be caged. The list is endless. When your finances are confined, you will find it tough to make or save money. You can try to get a job but remain jobless for years until God breaks the cage. And you receive freedom from such invisible spiritual pens.

When you have trouble completing a diploma or degree course, the chances are that the diploma or degree is in a cage. Often victims will get very frustrated and drop out of school. ***Any cage in any area of your life is broken now in Jesus' Name. Amen!***

August 14th

WORD OF THE ORACLE

[Revelation 3:12] *"He who overcomes, I will make him a pillar in the temple of My God, and he shall go out no more. I will write on him the name of My God and the name of the city of My God, the* **New Jerusalem,** *which comes down out of heaven from My God. And I will write on him My new name."*

NEW JERUSALEM [GREEK]: ***IEROSALEM KAINE***
The Greek term for 'New Jerusalem' is ***"Ierosalem Kaine,"*** as used in the above text-verse and in **[Revelation 21:2].** Strong's Concordance #2419, 2537:
The Greek term denotes "The Brand-New Jerusalem." The New Jerusalem that comes out of heaven is distinct from the earthly Jerusalem, the former Capital of Israel.
That is the city Abraham looked forward to, the city, whose builder and maker is God **[Hebrews 11:10].** That is the city that exists even now in heaven, for Paul calls it the Jerusalem that is above **[Galatians 4:26]**

<h1 style="text-align:center">Third Sunday in August</h1>

ONE YEAR BIBLE PLAN: PS 106-108/ROM 12:1-21

SUNDAY SCHOOL: ARE YOU A DISCIPLE OF JESUS? Part 3 of 4
THE REWARDS OF DISCIPLESHIP

#1. FUTURE BLESSINGS: We shall be saved from the wrath of God, which is to come **[Acts 17:31; Romans 5:9]**. We can look forward with joyful anticipation of eternity with God, free from sorrow, pain, and death **[Revelation 21:1-8]**.

#2. PRESENT BLESSINGS: Jesus offers a peace the world cannot give, to calm our troubled hearts **[John 14:27]**. His words inspire joy to lift our spirits out of depression **[John 15:11]**. Jesus offers us God's abiding love, which casts out fear **[John 15:9; 1st John 4:17-18]**. He makes it possible for us to become members of God's family **[Mark 10:28-30]**.

We could mention many other blessings that disciples of Jesus enjoy, but these suffice to demonstrate that though discipleship is costly, the rewards far exceed the cost!

Now that we understand discipleship's nature, cost, and rewards, we can now become faithful disciples of Jesus Christ.

But how does one begin? For the answer, we shall return in our next study to our text **[Matthew 28:19-20]**

August 16th

PREACH CHRIST

".... What then? Only that in every way, whether in pretense or truth, Christ is preached; and in this, I rejoice, yes, and will rejoice." **[Philippians 1:12-18]**

While in custody in Rome, Paul persisted in preaching the gospel of Christ to the extent that his imprisonment and the gospel were well known in the palace. His incarceration gave the brethren boldness to speak the word without fear. Paul never gave room to self-pity or despair; instead, he continued ministering while in custody. Like Joseph in prison, who was put in charge through his ministrations to other prisoners because the Lord was with him **[Genesis 39:20-23]**. In prison, Paul also wrote several Epistles, which form about one-third of his letters! What a robust management of time!

That is undoubtedly an encouragement to us as believers worldwide to preach Christ in every situation we find ourselves, whether at home, in the office, while traveling and in every marketplace. We must use every opportunity to propagate the gospel in love, especially in these times of tribulation around the world **[2nd Timothy 4:2]** as the coming of Christ draws near.

Prayer: *Lord, strengthen me in my spirit to preach the Gospel of Jesus Christ, no matter the challenges of life.*

TESTIMONY TUESDAY

THE HEAD AND NOT THE TAIL

"And the Lord shall make you the head, and not the tail……" **[Deuteronomy 28:13 AMPC]**

"It would be an understatement for me to say that I am happy with what God has done and still doing for me. Indeed, delightsome would be a better word to describe my feelings with the unusual breakthroughs. I had been working as an executive with one of the telecommunication giants for some time. Being a Christian who knew the covenant rights available to me, I desired a better position and income. I did not just wish it; I sowed continually for this promotion. Considering the variables, I did not know how or when the promotion would come. But I continued to sow towards my expectations. To the glory of God, a few weeks ago, I received a letter of promotion. To my greatest surprise and that of others, I received a double promotion! Thank you, Jesus!" Brother XYZ.

Are you in a position that you think is beneath your worth? Have circumstances placed you among the crowd? Do you think you should command more attention? I tell you; this is the time for you to stand out. You can no longer be part of the crowd because our God is great. *So, I charge you to take a step, of progress today because you are the head and not the tail in Jesus' Name. Amen!*

WEDNESDAY, August 18th

DEEP DIGGING: **ARE YOU A DISCIPLE OF JESUS? Part 4 of 4**

THE BEGINNING OF DISCIPLESHIP INVOLVES BAPTISM: Why baptism? **[Matthew 28:19]**. Remember, the goal of discipleship: Is to be like Jesus. He was Holy and sinless, yet we are to be like Him. And baptism is an act of faith that puts us in contact with the cleansing power in the Blood of Jesus to be forgiven **[Acts 2:38; Acts 22:16; Romans 6:3-4]**. It is also how we "puts on Christ" **[Galatians 3:26-8]**. So, baptism is the logical first step for true discipleship!
Baptism is an act of submission by faith in Jesus and repentance for our sins **[Acts 2:36-38; Acts 8:36-37]**.
Baptism is an act that involves burial in water, in which one then rises to walk in newness of life through the power of God **[Acts 8:38; Romans 6:3-4; Colossians 2:12]. That precludes infant baptism.** Because infants are incapable of believing and repenting. Sprinkling or pouring as a mode of baptism is not Biblical. For neither of these involve a burial nor an immersion [which is the meaning of the Greek word "baptizo"].

When Baptism is done according to God's Word, it is an act of faith on our part, which results in a beautiful working of God in our lives! Our sins are washed away by the Blood of Jesus **[Acts 22:16; Ephesians 5:25-27]**. We are regenerated and renewed by the Spirit of God so we can now live for God! **[Titus 3:5-6].** It is truly a rebirth involving both water and the Spirit **[John 3:5]**

<h2 style="text-align:center">BAPTISM INCLUDES FURTHER TEACHING
AND OBEDIENCE</h2>

Note what follows baptism in **[Matthew 28:20].** That brings us back to the very definition of discipleship. For Jesus clearly states: We are to be taught *[to be learners]* and observe *[to be adherents or doers].* Thus, we must embark on a life devoted to learning and doing all Jesus Christ commanded!

CONCLUSION: Only those who are scripturally baptized and demonstrating the marks of discipleship, despite the costs, can genuinely be called disciples of Jesus Christ!

Only then we can look forward to the rewards of discipleship and take comfort in Jesus' promise: *"And lo, I am with you always, even to the end of the age."* **[Matthew 28:20]**

Have you taken the initial steps in becoming a disciple of Jesus by faith, repentance, and baptism?

Are you becoming more like Him by demonstrating the marks of discipleship in your life in learning and in obedience...?

August 19th

GARMENT OF REPROACH

"... spake kindly to him and set his throne above the throne of the kings that were with him in Babylon, and changed his prison garments..." **[2nd Kings 25:28-30]**

In Biblical days, garment symbolizes positions. And as many as there are different apparel, so also are statues. You have a garment for beggars, lepers, prisoners, military attires, and attire for the rich, wealthy, and royal robe. Once you are identified with a misfit garment, you become a reproach and a miscreant in society. Beggars' garment is a license to beg, and prisoners' garment stands for the state's enemy. And a change of apparel from an attire of prisoners to ordinary garments signified freedom.

The devil has devised spiritual garments to humiliate humanity; these satanic garments are demonic marks place on victims to cause failures in their lives. **[Zechariah 3:1-4]** says, *".... Now Joshua was clothed with filthy garments and spake unto those that stood before him, saying, take away the filthy garments...."* Filthy garments represent shame, rejections, reproach, perennial failure, untimely death, lack and poverty, captivity, etc. But when God decides to change your situation for the best, He replaces these filthy garments with the garment of favor. ***God shall replace the filthy garment in your life with garments of blessings in the Name of Jesus Christ. Amen!***

August 20th

CARING MINISTRY

"But if anyone does not provide for his own, and especially for those of his household, he has denied the faith and is worse than an unbeliever." **[1ST Timothy 5:8-16]**

Paul's counsel to Timothy in **[1ST Timothy 5:8-16]** addresses one of the most severe pitfalls confronting Christians in Care Ministry. The Bible says, *"But if anyone does not provide for his own, and especially for those of his household, he has denied the faith and is worse than an unbeliever."* The family is an institution whose importance is emphasized all through Scripture. We cannot overlook the importance of the family. God gave us families as the building blocks of society and to learn how to care. However, caring for others to the detriment of our own families is a great disaster. Today, many focus all their attention on career, social engagement, extended family, ungodly company, leaving their nucleus families unattended.

Anyone who leaves his family uncared for is causing much havoc to society. Nothing is more pathetic than a committed believer who has become so concerned about caring for others that he or she forgets his own family. If you are guilty of this, you need to repent and have a change of heart today.

Prayer: *O Lord, help me be alive to my family's responsibilities in Jesus' Name. Amen.*

August 21st

WORD OF THE ORACLE

[Revelation 1:8] *"I am the **Alpha and the Omega**, the Beginning and the End," says the Lord, "who is and who was and who is to come, the Almighty."*

THE ALPHA AND THE OMEGA [GREEK]: *TO A KAI TO O*

The Greek term for The Alpha and The Omega' is *"To A Kai To O"* as used in the above text-verse and in **[Revelation 21:6; Revelation 22:13]**. Strong's Concordance #2532; 5598:

Alpha and Omega are the first and the last letters of the Greek Alphabet. In every context this phrase is used, it is difficult to tell whether the title applies to the Father or Christ or both.

Most likely, it can be attributed to both. God in Christ comprises everything that goes between the Alpha and the Omega, and the First and the Last. That expresses God's fullness, comprehensiveness, and all-inclusiveness. He is the Source of all things to their appointed end.

Prayer: *Holy Father, enlighten me in deep things of the spirit in the Name of Jesus Christ!*

Fourth Sunday in August

SUNDAY SCHOOL

THE GREAT COMMISSION ACCORDING TO MARK Part 1 of 6

[Mark 16:15-16] In Mark's account of "The Great Commission," the main thought of Jesus' command is: *"Go into all the world and preach the gospel to every creature"* **[Mark 16:15-16].** So, Jesus wants everyone to hear the gospel [the Good News].**You may have heard the gospel of Christ?** Or some part of the gospel. You might even have responded in some ways to it: But what exactly is the gospel of Christ? How should one respond to it? With Mark's account of the Great Commission, the gospel of Christ contains the following:

FACTS TO BELIEVE

1. THAT CHRIST DIED FOR OUR SINS: This is the main point Jesus had in mind when He said, *"Preach the gospel..."* which is fundamental to Paul's preaching **[1ˢᵗ Cor. 15:1-3]**

   a. Because we are all sinners! **[Romans 3:23].**

   b. And because the wages of sin is death! **[Romans 6:23].**

   c. In love, God offers His Son as a "propitiation" [sacrifice] for our sins! – **[1ˢᵗ John 4:9-10 AMP]**

happy sunday

August 23rd

WORTHY EVANGELIST

"After these things, the Lord appointed seventy others also and sent them two by two before His face into every city and place where He was about to go……." **[Luke 10:1-9]**

Saint Luke, the Physician, Evangelist, and the author of The Gospel According to Luke and The Acts of the Apostles, was devoted to what was profitable and productive. He was a Gentile **[Colossians 4:14).** He was not an eyewitness of the Ministry of Jesus from the beginning **[Luke 1:1-2].** Nonetheless, his contributions in spreading the gospel surpass many Jews, and disciples of Christ did. It does not matter what our background was before coming to Christ; all that the Lord is looking for is our willingness to be empowered for the work of the kingdom. We must remain faithful to the cause of the gospel in this depraved world. **[2nd Timothy 4:10-11].**

Jesus said to His disciples: *"Heal the sick and tell them, the kingdom of God is near..."* **[Luke 10:9; Psalm 147:3].** Like Dr. Luke, you can strengthen the weak and make bold those who are afraid with the Gospel **[Isaiah 35:3].** The Gospel is the medicine that cures sick souls. So, we must join in the spread of it to bring the perishing into the kingdom of God.

Prayer: *Father, grant that I may be devoted to what is right and live a productive life in Jesus' Name. Amen.*

TESTIMONY TUESDAY

PROFITABLE LABOR

"In all labor, there is profit: but the talk of the lips tendeth only to penury." **[Proverbs 14:23]**

Indeed, there is no labor in God's house that goes unrewarded. My testimony has proven that to me beyond all reasonable doubt. When I got the opportunity to serve the Lord as a chorister in one of OGIM churches in Maryland,' I embraced it with all my life. I put my God-given musical talents into the work to ensure that the work progressed. The commitment became very tough on me when I was moved out of state. Yet, I tried my best to ensure that; what was put in my care did not suffer. Severally, I traveled from my base in Virginia to conduct choir meetings and practices. As I did all these, the Lord continued to provide and cater to me. However, the icing on the cake for me was that I came out as one of the best with a merit award in my post-graduate degree. I thank God." Sister NG.

Beloveth, there is no labor on behalf of the Lord that goes unrewarded. What matters is God's assessment of your work. If your heart is right and you are faithful, God would eventually release the blessing. If you get the opportunity to serve, use it, and if not, please create one. Learn to sow your resources, talent to God's kingdom. ***Your labor in the house of God shall be profitable in Jesus' Name. Amen!***

WEDNESDAY, August 25th

DEEP DIGGING: **THE GREAT COMMISSION ACCORDING TO MARK Part 2 of 6**
OTHER FACTS OF THE GOSPEL TO BELIEVE:

1. Christ was raised from the dead, which is one fundamental of the gospel Paul preached **[1st Corinthians 15:4 AMP]**.
2. As also proclaimed by Peter in his first sermon in **[Acts 2:22-32]**.
3. Christ is exalted as King and Savior: He is now both Lord and Christ – **[Acts 2:33-36]**.
   He is head over all things **[Ephesians 1:20-23 AMP]**.
4. Christ is coming again: As promised when He ascended to heaven **[Acts 1:9-11]**. Coming to offer both rest to believers and tribulation to unbelievers **[2nd Thessalonians 1:7-10]**

He who died for us; rose and ascended to reign and will return in judgment! And whether we are prepared for His coming depends upon our obedience to the gospel **[2nd Thes. 1:8]**

In "The Great Commission According to Mark," it is clear the gospel of Christ contains.

1. FACTS TO BELIEVE. 2. COMMANDS TO OBEY AND WHAT IS TO BE BELIEVED? *Which we shall study in our next lesson.*

<h1 style="text-align:center">August 26th</h1>

ONE YEAR BIBLE PLAN: PSALM 139-141/ ROM. 14:1-23

MARK OF TESTIMONY

"..... and they came not for Jesus' sake only, but that they might see Lazarus also, whom he had raised from the dead." **[John 12:1-9]**

Some testimonies distinguish the recipients. When you receive such, you suddenly become a subject of attention. Before Lazarus's resurrection, little was known about him. In **[John 11:1],** he was described as a certain man of Bethany. The fact that his sisters were more known than him was evident, because their names were used to describe them. But after Jesus raised him from the dead, he became an instant celebrity. As people came from far and wide to see him. Beloveth, I do not know about you, but I still pray for God to release such testimonies upon my life. If you desire such testimonies, *I prophesy that your testimonies will mark you out in Jesus' Name. Amen!*

It is essential that you accept this prophecy. Because you cannot get what you do not accept, you cannot receive what you do not believe. That is why Jesus continually told Mary and Martha to believe. Today, he is telling you the same thing. Learn to believe and confess what you believe. Learn to believe that God is able and willing to bless you. As you do, you will enter the realm of breakthroughs where testimony is the watchword. Pray now!

Prayer: *My testimonies will mark me out in Jesus' Name!*

August 27th

STRENGHT FOR THE SAINTS

"Strengthened with all might, according to His glorious power, for all patience and longsuffering with joy." **[Colossians 1:11]**

A saint is anyone that is sanctified, a person consecrated and separated unto God's service, free from blemish. In **[Ephesians 1:1; Philippians 1:1],** Paul calls believers Saints. If in the assembly some were not saints, the epistle spur such to aspire to become one. Here are some saints' qualities mentioned: Faith, hope, and fruit in Christ; Love for other saints. **[Colossians 1:1-11].**

On hearing about the saints, Paul said: *"Giving thanks to God on their behalf and praying for them unceasingly that they might be filled with the knowledge of God's will in all wisdom and spiritual understanding. That they might walk worthy of the Lord unto all pleasing and be fruitful in every good work as they increase in the knowledge of God."*

That they might be strengthened with all might according to His glorious power unto all patience and long-suffering with joyfulness. Giving thanks unto the Father who has made us meet to be partakers of the saints' inheritance on high. Amen!

Prayer: *Lord, make me a saint!*

August 28th

WORD OF THE ORACLE

[Ephesians 3:2 AMPC] *"Assuming that you have heard of the __stewardship__ of God's grace (His unmerited favor) that was entrusted to me [to dispense to you] for your benefit."*

STEWARDSHIP [GREEK]: *"OIKONOMIA"*

The Greek term for 'Stewardship' is "Oikonomia," as used in the above text-verse and in **[1st Corinthians 9:17]**. Strong's Concordance #3622.

The word means "household management." In ancient times, the word was often used to describe the work of a person who took care of a large household or business **[Luke 16:1-2]**.

Paul was entrusted with the stewardship of God's economy, to dispense the riches of Christ to God's household, by preaching the Good News **[Ephesians 3:2-4 and Ephesians 3:11]**. Paul uses the same word to describe God's administration or the government of time **[Ephesians 1:10]**.

Fifth Sunday in August

SUNDAY SCHOOL: **THE GREAT COMMISSION ACCORDING TO MARK Part 3 of 6**

In "The Great Commission According to St. Mark" contains. **WHAT IS TO BE BELIEVED?**

1. **BELIEVE THE GOSPEL OF JESUS CHRIST:** We must believe the gospel, or we are lost! **[Mark 16:16]**. We must believe that the gospel is God's power for salvation to those who believe- **[Romans 1:16]**. E.g., we must believe that God raised Jesus Christ from the dead **[Romans 10:9-10]**. And for those willing to believe, eternal life can be theirs! **[John 3:16 *and* John 20:30-31]**.

2. **BE BAPTIZED FOR THE REMISSION OF SINS:** Jesus expected people to be baptized in response to His gospel **[Mark 16:15-16]**. Peter proclaimed a baptism for the remission of sins to those who believed **[Acts 2:37-38]**. Paul related the place baptism had in his salvation **[Acts 22:16]**. When we submit to baptism, God does His work in saving us! **[Colossians 2:11-13 AMPC]**.

happy sunday

August 30th

GOD'S FAITHFULNESS

".... They are new every morning: great is thy faithfulness. The LORD is my portion, saith my soul; therefore, will I hope in him". **[Lamentations 3:23-24]** **[2ⁿᵈ Timothy 2:13]** says, *"If we believe not, yet he abideth faithful: he cannot deny himself."* **[Romans 3:4]** says, *"God forbid: yea let God be true, but every man a liar..."* **[2ⁿᵈ Corinthians 1:20]** says, *"For all the promises of God in him are yea, and in him Amen, unto the glory of God by us."*

There is this testimony of a sister who came to a program, and the Word of God came and said *there is someone here who applied for a visa; it is already done.* She said Amen and was happy. She went to the embassy the next day. On arrival, the visa officer inspected her document and declined the application, and the sister said, but my pastor said it is done. The consular officer looked at her and said, who is your pastor? And she said: my father is the prophet. The visa officer then answered and said, even if your father is a Minister, a Governor, or a Commissioner, or the Pope, get out now before I call security. As the sister turned reluctantly to go, she said, but God said I had been granted the visa; at that point, the officer said I would give you the visa because you are so naive and funny. God has spoken. It is already settled. *I Prophesy God will speak in your favor henceforth in Jesus' Name. Amen!*

TESTIMONY TUESDAY

DELIVERED!

This testimony will edify you: *"For years, my father was oppressed by the devil with strange afflictions that defied all known medications. When he survived poisoning in 2014, it was not without some serious scares. Not long after the incident, he began to complain of strange movements all over his body. Whenever the movement starts, he would experience intense pains that made him groan and causes immobility. Since doctors could not diagnose any ailment, we were confused.*

We ran from pillar to post, here and there to no avail. Then I came with my Dad to the Oracle of God international ministries in one of the Communion and Healing service in Indian Head, Maryland, and during the service Pastor, Stevie said, as many as are sick here, you are already healed as you partake in the communion in Jesus' Name. Amen! To God be the glory, on our way home, my father began to vomit for about five minutes after that, all the pains and movement in his body was gone. Until this day, he never complained of the affliction again after that communion. Thank you, Jesus, Sister Agnes James.

Prayer: *Lord! Deliver me of all afflictions by the Blood of Jesus!*

WEDNESDAY, September 1ˢᵗ

DEEP DIGGING: **THE GREAT COMMISSION ACCORDING TO MARK Part 4 of 6**

3. **OTHER COMMANDS OF THE GOSPEL TO OBEY:** Is that we must confess our faith in Jesus Christ. Confessing with our mouth the Lord Jesus leads to salvation **[Romans 10:9-10]**. Jesus will confess us before God if we confess Him before others! **[Matthew 10:32-33]**.

4. *Repent of our sins:* Jesus Christ wanted repentance preached in His Name to all nations **[Luke 24:46-47]**. The Apostles, therefore, preached the need to repent **[Acts 2:37-38; Acts 3:19 AMPC; Acts 17:30-31]**.

5. **Be faithful unto death:** Faithfulness is necessary if we desire to receive the crown of life **[Revelations 2:10 TLB]**.

There is a real danger in losing our faith **[Hebrews 3:12-14]**.

When we obey the commands of the gospel, we receive beautiful blessings.

In "The Great Commission According to Mark," it is clear the gospel of Christ contains specific promises: we shall learn some more in our next lesson.

September 2nd

DELIVERANCE BY PRAISE
"…… Then shall the earth yield her increase……"
[Psalm 67:6-7]
In **[Acts 16:25-26],** Paul and Silas praised God, and the Lord sent an earthquake to deliver them. Their chains were broken, the gates of the prison fell flat. Do you desire deliverance? Praise God now!

PRAISE THE LORD NOW!
Lord! I give You all glory and honor. You are worthy of all my praise. Glory to Your Holy Name; I magnify Your Holy name. You are worthy of all adoration. You are the king of kings and the Lord of lords, the Ancient of Days, the I Am that I Am, the unchangeable Lord, the impossibility made possible God, You reverse the irreversible, You never sleep nor slumber. I blessed Your holy name! In Jesus' Name, I worship!

BIRTHDAY AND ANNIVERSARY PRAYERS!
Father, I commit September children and those celebrating their marriage this month into Your hands: this is the month of fruitfulness; let them be fruitful. Let their children be productive. Let them be fruitful physically, financially, materially, and spiritually in Jesus' Name. Amen!

September 3rd

UNPAYABLE DEBT

"Who gave Himself for our sins, that He might deliver us from this present evil age, according to the will of our God and Father." **[Galatians 1:4]**

Years ago, King Charles V was loaned a large sum of money by a merchant in Antwerp. The note became due, but the king was bankrupt and unable to pay. The merchant gave a great banquet for the King. When all the guests were seated and before the food was brought in, the merchant had a large platter placed on the table and a fire lighted on it. Then, taking the note out of his pocket, he held it in flames and burnt it.

The king threw his arms around his benefactor and wept. Just so, we have been mortgaged to God. The debt was due, but we are unable to pay. Two thousand years ago, God invited the world to the Gospel feast, and in the agonies of the Cross, God held our sins to the Cross until our guilt was killed. So, go ahead and thank Jesus for His sacrifice on the cross.

Prayer: *"In gratitude, I kneel before You, Lord Jesus Christ, for taking away all my sins upon you."*

September 4th

WORD OF THE ORACLE

[Romans 8:15] *"For you did not receive the spirit of bondage again to fear, but you received the Spirit of <u>**adoption**</u> by whom we cry out, "Abba, Father."*

ADOPTION [GREEK]: *"HUIOTHESIA"*

The Greek word for *'Adoption'* is *"Huiothesia"* as used in the above text-verse and in: **[Galatians 4:5 and Ephesians 1:5]** Strong Concordance #5206:

This Greek word for *'adoption'* is derived from the word ***"Huios,"*** meaning *'son,'* and the word ***"thesis,"*** meaning *'replacement.'* It is a legal term that, in this context, indicates that believers have the full privileges of sonship in God's family. Concurrent with this transference into sonship, God places the spirit of His Son into our hearts so that we become, in effect, His natural-born children.

So, we are not just *'adopted'* [in the sense of the word] but genuinely *'begotten'* by God. God makes children of men into children of God, just the reverse of what happened to Christ when the Son of God became the Son of man. Glory to God!

First Sunday in September

SUNDAY SCHOOL

THE GREAT COMMISSION ACCORDING TO MARK Part 5 of 6
PROMISES TO RECEIVE

THE PROMISE OF SALVATION: Clearly stated in Mark's account of the Great Commission **[Mark 16:16],** *"Whoever believes and is baptized will be saved, but whoever does not believe will be condemned."*

1. **This involves salvation from sin [Matthew 1:21]** *"And she shall bring forth a son, and thou shalt call his name Jesus: for he shall save his people from their sins.*

2. **We are promised the remission of sins! [Acts 2:38].** Our sins are "blotted out", "washed away" **[Acts 3:19; Acts 22:16].** Made possible by the precious blood of Christ **[Ephesians 1:7]**

3. **There is an ongoing blessing whenever we confess our sins – [1st John 1:9].** It also includes salvation from the wrath to come **[Romans 5:9]** when Jesus comes in flaming fire **[2nd Thessalonians 1:7-10].** A day of anger and indignation, tribulation, and anguish **[Romans 2:4-11]. *Such is the salvation that Jesus promises to those who obey the gospel!***

happy sunday

September 6th

GIFT OF PROPHECY

"And I fell at his feet to worship him. And he said unto me, See thou do it not: I am thy fellow servant, and of thy brethren that have the testimony of Jesus: worship God: for the testimony of Jesus is the spirit of prophecy." **[Revelation 19:10]**

[Acts 2:17 NIV] says, *"In the last days, I will pour out my Spirit on all people. Your sons and daughters will prophesy, your young men will see visions; your old men will dream dreams."* In **[Mark 5:24-34]**, the woman with the issue of blood prophesied to herself, *"if I can just touch the hem of the garment of Jesus, I will be made whole."* She said it to herself, and it came to pass. **[Joel 3:10]**, says *let the weak say I am strong.* You need to start prophesying strength, health, and wealth to yourself; it is acceptable to God. *Now declare I refuse to die poor, I refuse to die this year, I refuse to be a failure, I will reach my goal in Jesus' name. Amen!*

I prophesy every negative pronouncement against you will neither come to pass nor shall it be established in Jesus' Name. Amen! I want you to prophesy to yourself right now, mention your name, and say it will be well with me, I will not fail, I will not die but live, to declare the work and testimonies of God in my life, so shall it be in Jesus' Name. Amen!

Prayer: *I connect my spirit man to the Spirit of Christ, which is the Spirit of prophecy in Jesus' Name. Amen!*

TESTIMONY TUESDAY

".... out of their distresses. He sent his word and healed them...." **[Psalm 107:19-21]**

"I bless you, Lord, for granting your Prophet, your Oracle the 'Burden of Your Word' this script, "THE ORACLE OF GOD." As a minister of the gospel, I found this journal highly rewarding. I have experienced a new insight and powerful impartation from the very onset of using this book. I have since been buying copies for fellow pastors, counselees, counselors, and ministers of the gospel, and the testimonies are the same and much more. To God be all the glory, proven testimonies of signs and wonders have been recorded. Many have received healing, deliverance, and breakthroughs after studying, meditating, and praying with this book. Amen!" Min. Jake.

Rectifying inappropriateness that places people in satanic bondage is the essence of the gospel. In 'Today's word' above, when, and wherever an authentic sent-one speaks the sent word of God, there are always results without variables. God's Word goes with power and never returns void until its purpose is accomplished in our lives. Are you going through some terrible situations in your life? Are you disease-stricken? Is it loneliness in marriage, is it singleness, bareness, Joblessness? Are you debt-ridden; is your home foreclosed? *I prophesy the affirmation of the above testimony will be your confirmed testimony in Jesus' Name. Amen!*

WEDNESDAY, September 8th

DEEP DIGGING: **THE GREAT COMMISSION ACCORDING TO MARK Part 6 of 6 OTHER PROMISES OF THE GOSPEL TO RECEIVE:**

The Holy Spirit's Gift: Spoken of by Jesus Christ during His ministry **[John 7:37-39]**. Promised to those who repent and are baptized **[Acts 2:38-39; Acts 5:32; Galatians 3:26-27]**.

The Gift of Eternal Life: That we receive at the end of a fruitful life of holiness **[Romans 6:22-23]**. Reward to receive in the age to come **[Mark 10:29-30]**. And abundant life now as offered by Jesus **[John 10:10]**. Quality of life is made possible by our relationship with God **[John 17:2-3]**. A life in Christ enjoyed even now **[1st John 5:11-13]**.

Thus, the gospel has promised great blessings both in this life and the age to come! – **[1st Timothy 4:8 TLB]**

1. *The gospel Jesus wants His disciple to preach to every creature is the "Good News."*

2. *The facts to believe contains the message of God's love and grace.*

3. *The commands to obey are not challenging works done to earn salvation.*

4. *Acts of faith whereby we receive God's grace. To help us deal with the problem of sin and prepare us for the blessings of eternity!*

What have you done with the gospel of Christ thus far?

Jesus wants you to know about it, and you have heard it, and Christ made clear what He wants people to do about the good news:

       1.   To receive,
       2.   To believe it,
       3.   To be baptized,
       4.   Be discipled
       5.   And disciple others.

He also made clear what would happen if we do not:
    1.   *"He who does not believe will be condemned."*

Are you willing to believe the truth of the gospel and obey its commands?
If so, then its beautiful promises are there for you to receive in Jesus' Mighty Name. Amen!

September 9th

A BLESSING!

"...behold, thou shalt conceive in thy womb, and bring forth a son, and shalt call his name JESUS..." **[Luke 1:31]**

I believe God must have seen certain qualities in Mary that qualified her to be the vessel that will bring the Savior to the world. One of such attributes is her absolute faith in God's Word. Not many virgins would readily agree with a strange man [an angel] who came to tell them that they would conceive without a man. Many a lady would have either completely disagreed with the angel or outrightly curse him out for talking nonsense. But not Mary, as soon as she heard that the power of God should make her conceive, she said, *"Lord; be it unto me according to thy Word"* **[Luke 1:38]**. In other words, she simply said, Lord, I believe in you.

By so doing, Mary stretched her faith to take that which God was offering her. And she became blessed among women. *I prophesy you shall become a blessing to your generation.* God has decided to lift you like He did Mary. All He desires is for you to cooperate with Him by faith. Whatever you are dealing with now or the position you are in now does not matter. What matters is that you trust God. Once you do so, He will bring out that seed of greatness He has put in you and magnify it to benefit your generation. Today is a turning point in your life. *God will lift you to a position of relevance in Jesus' Name!*

September 10th

INVEST YOUR TALENT

"Every good gift and every perfect gift are from above and comes down from the Father of lights, with whom there is no variation or shadow of turning." **[James 1:17]**

God has endowed every man and woman with individual gifts, talents, and capabilities in His mercy and goodness. These are not to be used selfishly for our profit but His glory and the building of His kingdom. Our personalities, our intelligence, and our capabilities are gifts from His bountiful hand. If we divert their use for our profit, we become guilty of selfishness.

It is profitable for an employee or junior partner to work for the owner's profit and interest and glory. When the owner profits, all members of the firm profit.

So, as stewards of our talents, we should invest them for the glory and honor of the Almighty God. If God is glorified, we as His partners will be blessed. Our voices, our services, and our abilities are to be employed, primarily, for the glory of God.

Prayer: *Everything I have, you have given me, Father. Now give me the wisdom to use these gifts completely in Your will and to glorify Your Name. Amen!*

September 11th

WORD OF THE ORACLE

[Romans 8:29] *"For whom He foreknew, He also __predestined__ to be conformed to the image of His Son, that He might be the firstborn among many brethren."*

PREDESTINED [GREEK]: *"PROORIZO"*

The Greek word for *'Predestined'* is *"Proorizo"* as used in the above text-verse and in: **[Romans 8:30, Acts 4:28, 1st Corinthians 2:7, Ephesians 1:5 and Ephesians 1:11]** Strong Concordance #4309:

To predestine means *"to mark out beforehand," "to establish one's boundary, or one's limits, beforehand,"* The English word *'Horizon'* is a derivative of this Greek word.

God has fixed the Believer's ultimate destiny or horizon from all eternity: to be made like His Son, Jesus Christ. Note how the words *'predestined, called, justified, and mostly glorified'* in **[Romans 8:29-30]** are all in the past tense. That is because God, from His eternal perspective, sees this process as having been completed already.

From God's perspective, we have been glorified already because He sees us righteous because of the work of Jesus on the Cross. But still, in the march of time, we must undergo the process of being conformed to the image of God's Son.

Second Sunday in September 12th

SUNDAY SCHOOL: **BIBLICAL BAPTISM Part 1 of 7**

The necessity of baptism is evident in the Scriptures: Jesus commanded baptism in **[Matthew 28:19; Mark 16:16].**

1. His Apostles and teachers commanded baptism – **[Acts 2:38 *AMPC;* Acts 10:47-48].**

2. Many denominations practice some form of baptism yet vary in the mode of baptism [immersion, pouring, sprinkling]. The subject of baptizing infants, those not old enough to repent and believe, and the dead]; final baptism before death are satanic and unscriptural doctrines. There is only one Biblical purpose of baptism: to be saved, to show that one is saved. The Bible teaches that there is one baptism **[Ephesians 4:5].** Just as there is only One Lord, one faith, so, also, there cannot be different baptisms. Which raises several questions. Like one may have been baptized in some strange manner:

1. But was my baptism scriptural?
2. Was it the one baptism commanded by the Lord?
3. Then, should one be re-baptized or be scripturally re-baptized?

In our next lesson, we shall answer these questions and more:

Memory Verse: [Ephesians 4:5] *"One Lord, one faith, one baptism,"*

September 13th

CHECK YOUR THINKING!

"For as he thinks in his heart, so is he...." **[Proverbs 23:7]**

In **[Philippians 4:8],** Paul advised the Philippians to focus their thoughts on the positive because he understood the importance of man's thinking. He knew that our lives' outcome is a product of our ideas more than any other factor. What you are now is a product of your thoughts. If you think of fear, your life will be dominated by fear. If you think of failure, you will fail; you become successful if you think of success. To succeed in life, you must constructively focus on success. You must be success conscious, success-driven; you must make a conscious effort to reposition your consciousness and pattern it to achieve your heart's desire, to acquire it. When you understand this principle and doggedly apply it, you will walk through life with many accomplishments under your belt.

I do not know your desire in life, but you must try to regulate and direct your thought pattern to your destination if you desire to accomplish much in life. Do you want to prosper? Then think prosperity! Do you wish to be great? You need to think great! Is it healing you desire? Think healthy! Your mind is like a plot of fertile land, and your thoughts are the seed you sow in it, and what you sow is what you reap. *I prophesy that you will, from this day, plant great thoughts that will provoke a better future for you and your loved ones in the name of Jesus Christ!*

TESTIMONY TUESDAY

ONE YEAR BIBLE PLAN: S.O.S. 4-6/ 1 COR. 14:21-40

[Revelation 12:11] *"And they overcame him by the blood of the Lamb and by the word of their testimony...."*

OVERCOME BY YOUR TESTIMONY!

In **[1ˢᵗ Samuel 17:36-37]**, *"David said to Saul... thy servant slew both the lion and the bear..."* **[Proverbs 18:21]** says, *"Death and life are in the power of the tongue...."* David surely understood War of Words. That is why he made the battle with Goliath a battle of testimonies. Even when the giant tried to run him down psychologically by boasting that he would give his flesh to the birds of the air, David countered that declaration with the Name of the Lord in **[1ˢᵗ Samuel 17:44-45].** No wonder he defeated Goliath, the giant that sent shivers down the spine of King Saul, a seasoned warrior. Like David, you can overcome your problems with the words of your testimony. Has God done anything for you in the past? Has He delivered you from sickness, poverty, and death in the past? If so, say so! And He will deliver you again. So, whatsoever you are going through now has a solution in what you say. Begin to declare the testimonies of those things God has previously done for you against the situation you are facing now. As you do, those problems would melt like wax before the fire of God. *I prophesy you shall overcome the enemy by the words of your testimony in Jesus' Name. Amen!*

Prayer: *Lord, I praise Your name for the numerous testimonies I have seen in my life; I stand upon them and declare that every problem I am facing is temporary and will become testimonies speedily in Jesus' Name. Amen!*

WEDNESDAY, September 15th

ONE YEAR BIBLE PLAN: S.O.S. 7-8/ 1 COR. 15:1-17
**DEEP DIGGING: BIBLICAL BAPTISM Part 2 of 7
INSTANT OF RE-BAPTISM IN SCRIPTURE:**

THE DISCIPLES AT EPHESUS: Paul found some "disciples" at Ephesus **[Acts 19:1-5]**. He inquired as to whether they received the Holy Spirit when they believed **[Acts 19:2]**. In the context of the text verse, we can deduce that Apostle Paul had in mind the Holy Spirit's miraculous reception by the laying on of hands. **[Acts 19:6-7; Acts 8:17-19]**.

Their lack of knowledge regarding the Holy Spirit made Paul question their baptism **[Acts 19:2-3]**. Christ commanded baptism in the Name of the Holy Spirit: **[Matthew 28:19]**

How could they have been scripturally baptized if they had not even heard of the Holy Spirit? They had been baptized into John's baptism **[Acts 19:3]**. Paul explains that John's baptism was to prepare people for Christ **[Acts 19:4]**. Hearing the difference, they were baptized in the Name of the Lord Jesus **[Acts 19:5]**. Thus, we have an example of "re-baptism" in the New Testament.

They had been previously "baptized," but their baptism was lacking in some way even though it was baptism by immersion; and even though it was "for the remission of sins," it was still lacking **[Mark 1:4]**.

Their baptism was not in the Name of Jesus **[Acts 2:38; Acts 10:48; Acts 19:5]**.

And because their baptism lacked certain essential elements, "re-baptism" was necessary!

Nevertheless, we must not just spontaneously conclude or assume that our baptism lacks the essential element recommended by scripture, and so, we must consider whether "re-baptism" is necessary?

To determine whether "re-baptism" is required of us, we shall learn some of the elements of scriptural baptism in our next lesson:

September 16th

PURPOSE AND COMMITMENT!

"Not lagging in diligence, fervent in spirit, serving the Lord; rejoicing in hope, patient in tribulation, continuing steadfastly in prayer." **[Romans 12:11-12]**

As each generation becomes more addicted to the sedatives of life to dull the pain of living, the Almighty God is systematically moved to the back burner. Many are oppressed by a sense of triviality and thwarted purpose. Many more, men and women find no great goal or commitment to pull them and no inner stimulation to give meaning to their existence.

Nevertheless, Christ can still save you from the bane of boredom. He waits to give you a new sense of direction and to take dissatisfaction out of your life.

I recently spoke with a man who was recently converted to the Christian faith. This is what he said: *"I hadn't known what to do with my leisure time,"* he told me, *"but now I have a sense of commitment and purpose that I never knew before."*

If this is not your testimony, you need Jesus Christ indeed.

Prayer: *Even the smallest job I do today is part of my service to You, Lord. Father help my heart be so filled with Your Spirit to rejoice in whatever task is set before me in the Name of Jesus Christ. Amen!*

September 17th

PROMOTION

[1st Samuel 18:1-5] *".... And Saul set him over the men of war, and he was accepted in the sight of all the people and the sight of Saul's servants..."*

David's official address changed from the pasture of Bethlehem as a shepherd boy to the grand palace of King Saul, where he became a captain. Beloveth, I do not know how long you have been in the ghetto of life. Maybe you have done odd jobs all your life. Perhaps you do not have or know anyone who is highly placed to lift you. Perhaps life has treated you unfavorably thus far. Maybe you have lost all hope of making a decent living. This day the Lord has decided to change your situation. *So, I prophesy the Lord shall relocate you for unusual promotion in the Name of Jesus Christ. Amen!*

It does not take God much to change a man's situation. All He has to do is to orchestrate occurrences to provide opportunities for you to be favored. For David's sake, God arranged the defiance of Israel by Goliath. As soon as David saw and grabbed the opportunity, his situation changed. *The Lord is about to relocate you from the lower side to the upper side of life. So be prepared and be alert for the uncommon increase that is coming your way, be ready for great opportunities for personal advancement that will make themselves available to you; you shall be promoted this season in Jesus' Name. Amen!*

September 18th

ONE YEAR BIBLE PLAN: Isaiah 7-9/ 1st Cor. 16:1-12

[Romans 11:25] *"For I do not desire, brethren, that you should be ignorant of this **mystery**, lest you should be wise in your own opinion, that blindness in part has happened to Israel until the fullness of the Gentiles has come in."*

MYSTERY [GREEK]: *"MUSTERION"*

The Greek word for *'Mystery'* is *"Musterion"* as used in the above text-verse and **[Romans 16:25, 1st Corinthians 2:7, Ephesians 1:9, Ephesians 3:3, Ephesians 3:4 and Ephesians 3:9]** Strong Concordance #:3466

The word *'mystery,'* so often used by Paul, does not mean something incomprehensible, but something kept secret and now is open. In Paul's cultural and religious environment, the term was often used concerning the mystery religions.

Adherents to the mystery religions used the term to speak of their doctrine's secret knowledge revealed only to the initiated. In contrast, Paul uses the word to talk of a secret that is now open to all.

Prayer: *Holy Spirit, reveal unto me the mystery of the kingdom from your word this day in Jesus' Name. Amen!*

Third Sunday in September

SUNDAY SCHOOL: **BIBLICAL BAPTISM Part 4 of 7**

ELEMENTS OF SCRIPTURAL BAPTISM:

A. THE PROPER MODE: Baptism in the New Testament was a burial **[Romans 6:3]** *"Or don't you know that all of us who were baptized into Christ Jesus were baptized into his death?"* **[See also Colossians 2:12 AMPC]**

The Greek word baptizo means "to immerse, to plunge, to dip." "For 2000 years, baptism has been by immersion of the person underwater." "Baptism means immersion."

Unless it had been so, Paul's analogical argument about our being buried with Christ in baptism would have had no meaning nor make any sense. **[Romans 6:3].**

Nothing could have been simpler than baptism in its original form. When a convert declared his faith in Christ, he was taken at once to the nearest pool or stream of water and plunged into it, and henceforward he was recognized as one of the Christian communities. The Biblical mode of baptism is water immersion!

[Colossians 2:12] *"Buried with Him in baptism, in which you also were raised with Him through faith in the working of God, who raised Him from the dead.*

September 20th

DO ALL YOU CAN
"Who [with reason] despises the day of small things?"
[Zechariah 4:10 AMPC]

Do not be tempted to quit altogether because you are not where you wanted to be yet. Keep doing the little you can; soon, it will amount to some good. By doing the little you can, you will eventually work up to your place of blessing.

If you cannot exercise three days a week, but you can exercise once a week, then start with that and see what happens. You may find that doing what you can do will open the door to eventually for doing what you cannot do now! If you cannot study the Bible an hour every day, but you can for 10 -15 minutes, start with what you can do and watch it grow.

Many never get started with the little they can do because they want to start at the finish line. If you never get started in the right direction, you will never get to your destination. You may not be able to do everything but refuse to do anything! **[Philippians 4:13]**. *I prophesy the grace start doing your best upon you now in the Name of Jesus Christ!*

Prayer: *Lord, help me see the value of doing things that seem small and not getting discouraged when things take longer than I wanted or expected. Thank You for the strength to take baby steps of faith in Jesus' Name. Amen!*

TESTIMONY TUESDAY

NOT IMPOSSIBLE WITH GOD

"Behold, I am the Lord, the God of all flesh; is anything too difficult for Me?" **[Jeremiah 32:27]**

Do you ever feel weak and vulnerable? Do you have dreams that seem impossible? Do you ever worry about all the 'what ifs' and 'what thens' that probably won't even happen anyway?

I know what that is like declared a sister: Hear her!

Back in 2016, my husband and I had our first baby girl. After sixteen years of marriage and trying to be fruitful. We were, and still are, wholly overjoyed and so thankful to the Lord for our miraculous little gift. I have loved babies ever since I was two and always longed to be a mother one day.

Living with chronic illness, though, always seemed like have a baby is a distant dream. The enemy would sneer at me regularly, 'How could you ever be fit to be a mother? There's no possible way...' But we serve the living God – nothing is impossible for Him. "Behold, I am the Lord, the God of all flesh; is anything too difficult for Me?" [Jeremiah 32:27].

The Almighty God used Apostle Stevie Okauru, His Oracle, to fulfill His promise in our lives. Glory to God. Sister Rena.

 I prophesy you are next to testify to the miraculous!

WEDNESDAY, September 22nd

DEEP DIGGING: **BIBLICAL BAPTISM Part 5 of 7**
B. THE PROPER AUTHORITY IN WHICH BAPTISM MUST BE: "Biblically proper Baptism" must be in the Name of Jesus Christ **[Acts 2:38; Acts 10:48; Acts 19:5]**. By Jesus' authority, and not by any other, which would have been a baptism into the Name of the Father, the Holy Spirit, and the Son, as Jesus Himself commanded **[Matthew 28:19]** *"Go therefore and make disciples of all the nations, baptizing them in the name of the Father and of the Son and the Holy Spirit."* The Biblical Authority of Baptism is from Jesus Christ and no other!

 C. THE PROPER PURPOSE: Biblical Baptism was for the remission of sins **[Acts 2:38; Acts 22:16]**. It was made possible by one being buried with Christ into His death when baptized **[Romans 6:3; Colossians 2:12]**. That is the Apostolic tradition, maintained in the Churches of Christ. And it is an inherent principle, that without baptism no one can attain salvation and everlasting life. Baptism then has been instituted that it should lead us to the blessings [of this death] and through such death to eternal life. Therefore, we must be baptized into Jesus Christ and His death. **[Romans 6:3]** *"Or do you not know that as many of us as were baptized into Christ Jesus were baptized into His death?"*
The Biblical purpose of baptism is for the remission of sins!

September 23rd

HEARING GOD Part 1 of 3

"I cannot think of own mine self-do nothing: as I hear...." **[John 5:30]**

We are made to rest in God. In **[Genesis Chapters 1 and 2],** God finished the foundational work of creation and rested. His foundational work of creation is finished. **[Hebrews 4:9].** When God created the first Apple tree, He created seed in it so that all other Apple trees that would ever exist were worked into it. The same is with Man. After He created Man, God rested. Man's first full day was on the day of rest and God focused. So, when you align with God's plan, heaven's resources will come to your aid. Rest in God because life outside of God can be tiring **[Romans 8:28; Matt. 11:28-30].**

What does been a Christian mean to you? Is it following a system of Dos and Don'ts, or is it a relationship with God? If it is a fellowship of Dos and Don'ts, you will not make it because you are in for a struggle. Christianity is a relationship with God. Righteousness is a gift from God. Jesus said I would show you how to have real rest.

Let us yoke with God. Go at God's pace as He carries the yoke we just tag along. Live your life in obedience and alignment with the Father's plans and get God-sized results. God's voice is critical in living in rest as you hear God. God Bless you!

September 24th

HEARING GOD Part 2 of 3 Tips on hearing from God

"My sheep hear My voice, and I know them, and they follow Me." **[John 10:27]**

To hear from God, you must prioritize your relationship with Him over obeying rules set by Man. In **[John 5:18-19]** shows that Jesus does what the Father does. If you are going to walk with God, you must be flexible.

To hear from God, you must listen to Him. In communication, there are four skills; *read, talk, write, and listen!* When you speak, nothing happens, but when God talks, power flows. Listening is part of praying; take time to be quiet and let God speak to you. If you hear humans more than you hear God, your heart will be filled with fear instead of faith. Cut down on the noise of life and listen to the voice of God.

To hear from God is to be free from bias and prejudice. Nothing obstructs our capacity to hear God like selfishness. **[James 4:3-4; 1st John 2:17]**. You cannot approach God with bias or prejudice. If we were creators like our Father in heaven, we would have to rise above prejudice. **[Acts 10:34]** *".... In truth, I perceive that God shows no partiality."*

A lot of the things we do are traditional. We know what God said, but do we know what God is saying?

September 25th

WORD OF THE ORACLE

[Romans 12:2] *"And do not be conformed to this world, but be **transformed** by the renewing of your mind, that you may prove what is that good and acceptable and perfect will of God."*

TRANSFORM [GREEK]: *"METAMORPHOO"*

The Greek word for *'transform'* is *"Metamorphoo,"* as used in the above text-verse and in **[Matthew 17:2 and 2nd Corinthians 3:18]** Strong Concordance #:3339.

This Greek word means *"to change the form,"* as does the English derivative metamorphosis.

In the New Testament, this word is used to describe an inward renewal of our mind through which our inner spirit changes to the likeness of Christ. Paul told the Roman believers, *"Be transformed by the renewal of your minds"* **[Romans 12:2]**.

As our Christian life progresses, we should gradually notice that our thought life changes from Christ-lessness to Christlikeness. Transformation does not happen overnight. Our regeneration is not instantaneous but continuous. We are progressively conformed to Christ's image as we spend time in intimate fellowship with Him **[2nd Corinthians 3:18]**.

Fourth Sunday in September

SUNDAY SCHOOL
BAPTISM BIBLICAL Part 6 of 7

D. THE PROPER SUBJECT: Baptism was commanded of those capable of repentance **[Acts 2:38]**. Baptism was permitted for those who possessed faith **[Acts 8:37; Mark 16:16]**.

What about infant baptism? "Infant Baptism cannot be proved by Scriptures that it was instituted by Christ or begun by the first Christians nor by the Apostles." "Infant baptism was established neither by Christ nor the Apostles. In all places where we find the necessity of baptism, either in a dogmatic or historical perspective, it is evident that it was only meant for those who can comprehend the word preached and of those being converted to Christ by an act of their own will."

The Biblical subject for baptism is for a penitent believer! Remember, when one element was lacking, "re-baptism" was commanded in **[Acts 19:1-7]**. In that case, it was despite having the proper mode, purpose, and subject!

Having surveyed the essential elements of scriptural baptism, we shall consider some Biblical cases in our next lesson:

Memory Verse: [Acts 2:38] *"Then Peter said unto them, Repent, and be baptized every one of you in the name of Jesus Christ for the remission of sins, and ye shall receive the gift of the Holy Ghost."*

<h1 style="text-align:center">September 27th</h1>

[Ephesians 3:17 TLB] *"And I pray that Christ will be more and more at home in your hearts, living within you as you trust in him. May your roots go down deep into the soil of God's marvelous love."*

HEALTHY FRUITS!

When you become a student of God's Word, you begin to desire a change in your behavior. But, as soon as you deal with one bad behavior, another immediately pops up to replace it. Why? Because rotten fruit comes from an evil root.

For example, if we feel bad about ourselves, we will produce bad fruit of some kind. Such as anger, insecurity, fear, and indecision tend to show up in our behavior. And we must deal with the source. No matter how good things look outwardly, if they are not right on the inside, they will be revealed on the outside sooner or later.

Your worth and value are not based on outward things; they are based on God's love for you. Receive His love, learn to love like Him, and value yourself, and you will begin to produce better fruits in your life in Jesus' Name. Amen!

Prayer: *Father, help me to have a greater understanding of Your love. Help me see myself the way You see me and receive my worth and value from You in Jesus' Name. Amen!*

TESTIMONY TUESDAY

I PROFESS MY DAY

"... The Lord said, "Go ahead and anoint him. He is the one." Samuel took the flask of olive oil and anointed David...." **[1ˢᵗ Samuel 16:11-13 GWT]**

Today, God still chooses people for divine promotion. So, the story of David is not over unique. "There is this story of a young lady that is like that of King David's: *"According to her, several of them were chosen for a position in an establishment: In her estimation, she was the least qualified. Even on receipt of a favorable prophecy concerning divine promotion, she still did not expect the miracle. Then came the appointed day; every other candidate was at least forty-five minutes late, so since she was the only one that came on time, she was given the position without any further interview. The others who were much more qualified were turned down for lateness. So, you can see that God is still lifting people He loves with His loving hands."*
Do you desire to be elevated by God as he did with David and the Lady in the above testimony? All the Lord wants from you is to trust and obey His instructions, for there is no other way to be happy and lifted in Jesus Christ but to trust and obey Him.

Prayer: *Lord, give me the grace to trust and obey you entirely in the Name of Jesus Christ. Amen!*

WEDNESDAY, September 29th

DEEP DIGGING: **BAPTISM BIBLICAL Part 7 of 7**
4. WHEN RE-BAPTISM IS NECESSARY

1. **IF OUR BAPTISM INVOLVED THE WRONG MODE:** Pouring or sprinkling as practiced by Catholics, Lutherans, Presbyterians, Episcopal, Methodists, and others. When our baptism lacked the proper mode [immersion], "Re-baptism" would, therefore, be necessary.
2. **IF OUR BAPTISM INVOLVED THE WRONG AUTHORITY:** If we were baptized by the authority of anyone other than Jesus Christ: Such as Ellen G. White [Seventh Day Adventists], The Watch Tower Society [Jehovah's Witnesses], Joseph Smith [Mormons], and others. If our baptism were not by the only proper authority [Jesus Christ], "Re-baptism" would, therefore, be necessary.
3. **IF OUR BAPTISM INVOLVED THE WRONG PURPOSE:** If we were baptized as a public confession of faith [thinking we were already saved] as practiced by most Baptists, Assemblies of God, and many others. If our baptism were not for the right purpose, [remission of sins] "Re-baptism" would be required to ensure we have been scripturally baptized.
4. **IF OUR BAPTISM INVOLVED THE WRONG SUBJECTS:** If baptized, but we were not penitent believers.

As is the case when people are baptized when all their friends are they doing it or because their spouse, fiancé, or parents are pressuring them to do it [and they do it to please them, not God].

If we were baptized in infancy, because infants were incapable of faith or repentance, our baptism lacked the right subjects [penitent believers]. Our need for "re-baptism" would be just as great!

CONCLUSION: Remember, there is only one baptism **[Ephesians 4:4-5]**. Baptism commanded by the authority of Jesus Christ **[Matthew 28:18-19; Mark 16:16]**. Baptism is for the remission of sins **[Acts 2:38; Acts 22:16]**. Baptism, symbolizes a burial, an immersion in water **[Acts 8:38; Acts 10:47-48; Romans 6:3; Colossians 2:12]**

Baptism requires a penitent believer **[Acts 2:38; Acts 8:37.**

The aim of this study is not to unduly trouble one's assurance of salvation. But to make our calling and election sure **[2nd Peter 1:10 AMPC]**.

And to examine whether we are genuinely in the faith **[2nd Corinthians 13:5 TLB]**. Because of the many baptisms taught and practiced in the religious world, we must never hesitate to ask, *"Is our Baptism Scriptural or Biblical?"*

If not, then as Ananias told Saul of Tarsus: *"...why are you waiting? Arise and be baptized, and wash away your sins, calling on the Name of the Lord."* **[Acts 22:16]**.

September 30th

HEARING GOD Part 3 of 3 Tips on hearing from God

"I cannot think of own mine self-do nothing: as I hear, I judge: and my judgment is just; because I seek not mine own will, but the will of the Father which hath sent me."
[John 5:30]

Hearing from God is foundational to our living and resting in Him. Our lives were designed to walk with God in a state of rest. And the principle of rest was incorporated into the creation story. God worked for six days and rested on the seventh, and since then, He has designed for us to live in His rest. Living in His rest is living in alignment with the foundation that He laid.

In **[John 5:19],** we see that Jesus was yoked with God the Father. He never did anything outside what the Father told Him to do. Every time Jesus took a step-in alignment with God, a miracle occurs, and that's how God designed for us to live.

To hear from God, we must read and meditate on the scriptures. It helps us to acquire God's vocabulary. **[2nd Timothy 3:16-17].** The scriptures teach us what God says and what God will not say. It teaches us what is right and what is wrong. So, you must train your system to receive from God by reading and meditating His Word. You would then find out that God wants to speak to you; He uses scriptures to speak to us.

You will then begin to feel differently as God speaks to you directly from specific scripture. The more you want to know and understand God, the more you should fill yourself with God's vocabulary. **[Joshua 1:8, Psalm 1:1-**

2]. Fill your spirit, soul, mind, and imagination with scriptures non-stop.

To hear from God, always watch out for spontaneous thoughts, pictures, or texts. God is Spirit and can speak to you through your thoughts and ideas. **[John 4:24; Luke 24:27-32].**

Revelation usually comes with sensation. One of the ways you know it is God speaking to your senses; the thought may not align with your logical frame of thoughts, and the result will be different and unique. Your system responds differently when what is coming to you is from God.

God speaks through His prophets. [Amos 3:7]. He speaks through His prophets and gives them extraordinary gifts for intuition. **[Ephesians 4:11].** In the New Testament, every Christian can prophesy. So, do not open yourself to confusion. What someone says should be confirmed.

To hear God is to place your receiver on the right frequency. [Job 32:8].

Inspiration is the key to revelation. [Ephesians 5:18].

Music is also essential, as is reading **[2nd Kings 3].**

Put your equipment at the right frequency or on the faith channel. **[Hebrews 11:6].** If you put yourself in the frequency of negativity, you will not hear anything from God.

October 1ˢᵗ

[Hebrews 13:15] *"...let us offer the sacrifice of praise to God continually...."*

GRACE TO PRAISE!

We can never praise God enough. We can pray amiss, but we can never praise amiss. That we are alive today is simply by the grace of God. We are not better or smarter than anyone dead. So, let us praise God. Let us humble ourselves before the Almighty God now, worship Him.

PRAYER OF PRAISE AND THANKS:

Eternal Rock of Ages, the Alpha, the Omega, the Unchangeable Lord, The Holy One of Israel, the Lion of the tribe of Judah, the Bright and Morning Star, I bless Your holy Name. You are higher than the highest, better than the best, older than the oldest, wiser than the wisest, more potent than the strongest, glory is to Your holy Name. Accept my worship in Jesus' Name!

BIRTHDAY AND ANNIVERSARY PRAYER!

October is the tenth month of the year; ten is two times five, so ten is the number for double grace. Father, I thank You for Your children born in October and those wedded and wedding this month. Thank You for preserving their lives. Lord, release upon them double grace, let their blessings be doubled in all areas of their lives in Jesus' Name. Amen!

<h1 style="text-align:center">October 2nd</h1>

WORD OF THE ORACLE

[Romans 15:13] *"Now may the God of **hope** fill you with all joy and peace in believing, that you may abound in hope by the power of the Holy Spirit."*

HOPE [GREEK]: *"ELPIS"*

The Greek word for *'Hope'* is *"Elpis"* as used in the above text-verse and in: **[1st Corinthians 9:10]** Strong Concordance #1680: This Greek term denotes *"confident expectation"* or *"anticipation,"* not *"wishful thinking"* as in common phrasing.

The use of the word *'hope'* in this context is unusual and ironic, for it suggests that the Gentiles, who knew nothing or little about the Messiah, were anticipating His coming.

However, we need only to think of Cornelius in **[Acts 10]** to realize that some Gentiles had anticipated the coming of the Jewish Messiah, for Jesus was sent, not only for the salvation of the Jews but also for the Gentiles. Since God is the Author of our salvation, we can call Him the God of hope, for He has given us hope **[Romans 15:13]**.

Prayer: *Lord God of hope, fulfill all my hope and expectation for my life in your Word in the Name of Jesus. Amen!*

First Sunday in October

SUNDAY SCHOOL: **AFTER BAPTISM Part 1 of 3** Wonderful blessings come to those who respond to the gospel of Christ in baptism. They receive remission of sins and the gift of the Holy Spirit **[Acts 2:38-39]** *"....Repent and be baptized, every one of you, in the name of Jesus Christ, for the forgiveness of your sins. And you will receive the gift of the Holy Spirit.....*" We experience a washing of regeneration and renewal by the Holy Spirit after Baptism **[Titus 3:5-7]**.

Indeed, by God's grace, we are "saved." Saved from past sins **[Mark 16:16]**. With sins washed away by the Blood of Jesus **[Acts 22:16; Ephesians 1:7]**. We become heirs according to the hope of eternal life **[Titus 3:7]**.
Yet, in another sense, we are still to be "saved." We must make our call and election sure **[2nd Peter 1:10]**. We must be careful to retain our salvation **[1st Timothy 4:16]**. We must remain faithful to receive the crown of life **[Revelation 2:10]**.

What are we to do after Biblical Baptism that will ensure remaining faithful to God?
There are some: We shall study them in our next lesson:

Memory Verse: [Mark 16:16] *"Whoever believes and is baptized will be saved, but whoever does not believe will be condemned."*

October 4th

TOTAL RECOVERY

"Then he went down and dipped himself seven times in the Jordan, as the man of God had said, and his flesh was restored...." **[2nd Kings 5:14 AMPC]**

There is hardly anybody who has not lost one thing or the other. Some are not as healthy as they use to be, some can no longer see as clearly as they use to, some are not as wealthy and comfortable as they use to be, some are no longer hot for the Lord as they used to. *But I prophesy total recovery of everything you have lost in Jesus' Name!* **[Joel 2:25-26 AMPC]** says, *"And I will restore unto you the years that the locust has eaten--the hopping locust, the stripping locust...."*

Recovery implies that you had something, you lost it, and then you got it back. In **[2nd king 6:5-7]**, the prophet's sons were cutting down trees by river Jordan, and the ax head they were using fell into the river, and they recovered it by the anointing of the prophet. *I decree in the Name of the Lord, everything you have lost; I command total recovery in Jesus' Name. Amen!*

In **[2nd kings 5:14]**, when Naaman deep himself into Jordan the seventh time, his skin was restored to him like the skin of a newborn child. In other words, there was no sign left that he ever had leprosy. *I prophesy, by the time God finishes with you, nobody will know you ever had a problem in Jesus' Name!*

TESTIMONY TUESDAY

EXCELLENT SPIRIT

"...... And in all matters of wisdom and understanding that the king enquired of them, he found them ten times better than all...." **[Daniel 1:17-20]**

"God has just proven to me that the principle of seed faith can be used to get anything at all from Him. When I gained admission into the university, I desired to become an excellent student. Consequently, I began to sow seeds of faith continuously to put heaven on my side. Things went on well until I was afflicting temporary amnesia, i.e., temporary loss of memory. But continuous prayers and ministrations restored my memory. Glory to God!

After the attack, I became more dogged in my study; besides, I always sowed and confessed God's Word concerning excellence and intellect. To the glory of God, this year, I graduated with a first-class degree in my discipline. And to crown my joy, I won a post-graduate scholarship to study at the prestigious Cambridge University, England." Sister Tisha.

Wow! What a testimony! Do you desire the excellent Spirit of God? *Receive it now in Jesus' Name.* Like Sister T, I was an outstanding student. That spirit has affected everything I do. So, as an Oracle of God, I am empowered to release it on others. *Thus, I prophesy, the spirit of excellence is released upon you now. Go and excel in all you do in Jesus' Name. Amen!*

WEDNESDAY, October 6th

DEEP DIGGING: **AFTER BAPTISM Part 2 of 3**
THINGS TO REMEMBER

1. **YOU ARE A NEW CREATURE:** By being in Christ **[2nd Corinthians 5:17]**. We have been raised with Christ to walk in newness of life **[Romans 6:3-4]**.

2. **YOU ARE A BABE IN CHRIST**: We begin our new life as "babes in Christ" **[1st Cor. 3:1-2]**. We start with spiritual "milk." God enables us to grow in due time! **[Heb. 5:12-14]**.

3. **YOU ARE IN A CRITICAL PERIOD:** As a babe, we can easily be "tossed about" **[Ephesians 4:14-16]**. Satan often strikes hardest at the beginning of our walk with God, e.g., **[Matthew 4:1-11]**. He loves to see s fail! **[1st Peter 5:8]**.

4. **YOU FACE THE POSSIBILITY OF FALLING:** If we allow ourselves to be hardened by the deceit of sin **[Hebrews 3:12-14]**; especially when we think we are secure **[1st Corinthians 10:12]**. But God can be trusted to help us through temptations **[1st Corinthians 10:13; 1st John 2:1-2]**.

5. **YOU ARE TO BE A GOOD EXAMPLE:** An example of those who believe **[1st Timothy 4:12]**. An example in deeds and words **[Titus 2:7]**. Others should look to you as to how to live for Christ **[Philippians 3:17]**. Remembering such things will undoubtedly help keep one firm in the faith:

<h1 style="text-align:center">October 7th</h1>

HEARING AND SEEING Part 1 of 2

"I will stand at my watch and station myself on the ramparts; I will look to see what he will say to me and what answer I am to give to this complaint." **[Habakkuk 2:1]**

When we hear from God, we are expected to see some things. God's Word, the Scripture, is meant to communicate pictures. It is the picture of Scripture that is called revelation **[1st Samuel 3:21]**. As God says it, you must see it, to be it. If you only hear it or read it, it is information; when you move from information to revelation, you experience the manifestation of your expectation. **[Jeremiah 1:11-12]**

Every time revelation is born, a manifestation is inevitable! **[Matthew 8:16-17]**. When we hear from God, God expects us to see things [revelation], and when we see those divine things, God expects us also to hear them **[1st Kings 4:33-34; Proverbs 24:30-34; Jeremiah 18:1-6]**.

In the realm of the Spirit, you must be observant: Observation is key to receiving instruction and divine direction. Observation facilitates discretion that brings wisdom. Be alert to hear and see your blessings manifest as expected in Jesus' Name!

<u>Prayer:</u> *Father, thank You for Your Word to me today. To You be all the glory Lord, in Jesus' Name. Amen!*

HEARING AND SEEING Part 2 of 2

"The Word of the Lord came to me saying, "What do you see, Jeremiah?" And I said, "I see a rod of an almond tree." Then the Lord said to me, "You have seen well, for I am watching over My word to perform it." **[Jeremiah 1:11–12]**

What do I learn from what I see? What instruction and direction do I get from what I see? How much wiser am I from what I see and hear? These are questions we must ask ourselves.

God is always speaking, but men are not still listening **[Psalm 19:2-3]**. Many hear but see nothing, and many see but hear nothing, so life situations never change. It is not what you heard or read that matters most, but what you see from what you hear and what you hear from what you see. When what you hear translates into what you see and what you see translates into what you hear, then the person you used to be will translate into the one you are meant to be!

Therefore, you must pray and ask God to give you seeing eyes and hearing ears **[Proverbs 20:12; Psalm 119:18; Ephesians 1:16-18]**. Be determined and diligent to hear and see and to see and hear **[Habakkuk 2:1-2]**. There is a deliberate dimension to it. God does not do serious things will unserious people. God does not give insight to the one that has no interest. There is no future for the plan-less person. **[2nd Timothy 2:15]**.

If you want to make a mark on the time, hit the road on time. Document what you see and hear **[Habakkuk 2:2;**

Mark 4:24; 1ˢᵗ John 1:3-4]. God does not waste instruction. The observation you made on the road, write it down, do not wait until you get home. *"The faintest ink is more powerful than the strongest memory." "The best time to make hay is when the sun shines" "The best time to strike the iron is when it is hot." "The best time to pen the thought is when it arrives."*

There is a connection between the thought in your head and the pen in your hand. When you pen your thoughts, you pull in more. There is a connection between inspiration and documentation. When you document your thoughts, it will pull out more and make God entrust you with more. Do not allow your spiritual senses of hearing and seeing to be wasted.

Prayer: *Father, open my eyes to see as I hear and open my ears to hear as I see, in Jesus' Name. Lord, I receive the determination and the diligence to listen to and see, in Jesus' Name. I welcome the discipline to apply what I hear and see, from documentation to application, in Jesus' Name. Father, I ask that as I learn, help me see and listen to what I am experiencing. Reveal Yourself to this generation in this season. Let us hear what we are meant to hear, see what we are to see, and know what we are to understand, Oh Lord, in Jesus' Name. Amen!*

October 9th

WORD OF THE ORACLE

[1st Corinthians 1:9] *"God is faithful, by whom you were called into the **fellowship** of His Son, Jesus Christ our Lord."*

FELLOWSHIP [GREEK]: *"KOINONIA"*

The Greek word for *'Fellowship'* is ***"Koinonia"*** as used in the above text-verse and in **[Acts 2:42, Philippians 2:1 and 1st John 1:3-7]** Strong Concordance #2842: This Greek word means *"that which is shared in common."* In the New Testament, the word is used to denote the believers' joint participation in the Triune God: God the Father, God the Son, and God the Holy Spirit.

The father and Son have enjoyed communion with each other before the creation of the world. When the Son was on the earth, His fellowship with the Father also came with Him. During His ministry days, he introduced the Father to His disciples and initiated them into this fellowship. Once the disciples were regenerated, they entered fellowship with the Father and the Son by the Holy Spirit. The unique connection between the Father and the Son that began in eternity was manifested in time through the Son and was introduced to the Apostles, and then through the Apostles was extended to each believer through the indwelling of the Holy Spirit **[2nd Corinthians 13:14 and Philippians 2:1].**

Second Sunday in October

SUNDAY SCHOOL: **AFTER BAPTISM Part 3 of 3**
THINGS TO DO

1. **PUT GOD FIRST IN ALL THINGS:** Love Him with all your being **[Matthew 22:37]**. Seek first His kingdom and its righteousness **[Matthew 6:33]**. Remain faithful!
2. **STUDY THE WORD OF GOD:** Long for the Word, like an infant long for milk **[1st Peter 2:2]**. Emulate the Bereans believers in their attitude towards the Word **[Acts 17:11]**. Receive the Word with meekness, and it will save you! – **[James 1:21]**.
3. **BE FERVENT IN PRAYER ALWAYS:** Jesus made it possible to approach God's throne directly by His Name **[Hebrews 4:14-16]**. Wonderful blessings come through prayer **[Philippians 4:6-7]**. Be devoted to prayer, with an attitude of thanksgiving **[Colossians 4:2]**.
4. **BE DILIGENT IN ASSEMBLING AND IN FELLOWSHIP WITH OTHER BELIEVERS:** We must not forsake the assembly of saints **[Hebrews 10:24-25]**. It is a time for fellowship, prayer, worship, and for the Lord's Supper **[Acts 2:42; Acts 20:7; 1st Corinthians 11:23-26]**. Neglecting the assemblies is a symptom of spiritual stagnation and retrogression!

HELP SAVE OTHERS; THROUGH SOUL WINNING EFFORT: The Lord wants His disciples to make more disciples **[Matthew 28:19-20]**. Those diligent in saving others are more likely to remain saved **[1st Corinthians 9:19-27]**. If you lose your enthusiasm for saving souls, you may lose your salvation!

CONCLUSION: These are things to remember and do that may help the recently baptized, not just for new Christians, for any Christian. And believers who have left their "first love" **[Revelation 2:4]?** For they should "repent and do the first works" **[Revelation 2:5]**.

These are some of the "first works" that one needs to do.
Are you in need of doing the "first works"?
Perhaps you even need to obey the "first steps" of the gospel of Christ. **[Mark 16:16; Acts 2:38; Acts 22:16]**

happy sunday

October 11th

GOD' MERCY

"For He saith to Moses, I will have mercy on whom I will have mercy, and I will have compassion on whom I will have compassion." **[Romans 9:15]**

God is more than enough. He is unlimited in resources, unlimited in love, endless in generosity, boundless in mercy. *May you experience the infinite mercy of the Most High God today in the Name of Jesus Christ. Amen!*
[Ephesians 2:4-5] says *God is rich in mercy; part of his wealth is mercy.* **[Psalm 103:11]** says *as heaven is far from the earth,* so is His mercy to those who fear Him.
In **[Mark 1:40-45],** a leper came to Jesus and said I know you can cleanse me if you will, and Jesus said I am willing, so He touched the leper, and the leper received his healing. The bible says He was moved by compassion. Whenever His mercy overtakes Him, He does things He will never have done ordinarily. God is the One who says you must not touch a leper, that when you do, you will be unclean, but when his mercy gripped Him, He touched the leper. When blind Bartimaeus ask Jesus for mercy, Christ had compassion on him, and his sight was restored. Are you in captivity? The Lord will have mercy on you, and you will testify in Jesus' Name. Amen!
Prayer: *O God, let me experience the result of Your mercy!*

TESTIMONY TUESDAY

"When people are brought low, and you say, 'Lift them!' then he will save the downcast." **[Job 22:29 NIV]**

A DIFFERENT TESTIMONY

There is a global economic recession in the world today because of the global pandemic of Covid-19. Companies and businesses are closing; there is a general economic meltdown worldwide. But the scriptures depicted a different scenario for us in **[Job 22:29].** *For the believers:*

A couple of weeks ago, a brother declared he believe in this same prophecy and had this wonderful testimony below: *"I woke up this morning, down in my spirit. I had many things planned out for the impending trip with my family but with no funds. Depressed, then suddenly, I remembered that I had an appointment with the man of God. So, I went with great expectation, as the man of God prayed, he prophesied and declared, "Enter into your season of financial breakthrough and financial favor." The same day, I received a call from a friend; he said he is right in front of my home with some money for me. I was amazed when I opened the bulky envelope. It was three times the amount he had promised me."* Brother YJ.

Do you desire such testimony? *Receive it now as I prophesy; it is your season of financial favor in Jesus' Name. Amen!*

Prayer: *I enter my season of financial favor today!*

WEDNESDAY, October 13th

DEEP DIGGING: **THE GREAT COMMISSION ACCORDING TO LUKE Part 1 of 5 REPENTANCE**

In Luke's account of "The Great Commission" **[Luke 24:44-47]**, we see that Jesus wants two things to be preached in His Name to all nations. *What are those two things?* **A. Repentance, b. Remission of sins.**

In the book of Acts, the Apostles did indeed preach repentance and remission of sins. In the preaching of Peter in **[Acts 2:38; Acts 3:19]**. The word refreshing refers to the restoration of strength and nourishment. Strength is restored when hope is restored.

Repent and be converted. To be converted is to change your thinking, reset your mindset, and change your attitude towards Jesus Christ and serve Him in Spirit and truth. **[Acts 5:31].** Also, in the preaching of Paul **[Acts 13:38; Acts 17:30].**

Do we understand what it means to repent? Do we appreciate what it means to have our sins remitted?

To be sure that we do, we shall examine both concepts in our next lesson:

Prayer: *Lord, give me the understanding of the great commission!*

October 14th

PREFERRED

"... Daniel was preferred above the presidents and princes because an excellent spirit was in him...."
[Daniel 6:3]

Have you taken time to ask yourself why certain people go through life with much ease while others struggle through life only barely make a living? Have you ever wondered why some people always have good news for themselves and their families? While others have tales of woes and calamities. Are you aware that sometimes certain people are chosen above others for no special reason? Do you know why these things happen? There is one word that is responsible for these happenings. Favor! According to the Oxford Advanced Learner's Dictionary, favor is a treatment that is generous to a person or a group of persons in a way that seems unfair to others.

This is especially true when the favor is from God. Divine favor supernaturally orchestrates spiritual and physical circumstances to impact your life positively and favorably. That is why Daniel was preferred above his peers. When God favors you, people tend to favor you without any solicitation. Do you want to experience the favor of God that Daniel had? *Place your right hand over your head now and pray thus:*

Prayer: *The grace to be preferred fall upon me now in Jesus' Name. Amen!*

October 15th

".... And how she was healed immediately. And he said unto her, Daughter, be of good comfort: thy faith hath made thee whole. Go in peace." **[Luke 8:47-48]**

REPROACH REMOVED!

For twelve years, the woman with the issue of blood in **[Luke 8:43-48]** lived like an outcast. Having spent all her earnings on doctors without getting well, she decided that Jesus was her last hope. She believed with all her heart that she will receive her healing if she touches the hem of Jesus's garment. And it happened according to her faith. *".... Immediately, her issue of blood stanched."* **[Verse 44].**

Your issue of concern may not be an issue of blood. It may be that you have been unable to get married. It may be poverty, sickness, barrenness, joblessness, singleness. Whatever it is, *I decree now; your reproach is removed in Jesus' Name!*

Therefore, rejoice because shame comes to an end today in your life in the Name of Jesus. "Faith is the active response of the human spirit to God's Word." How you respond to this prophecy determines what you get from it. *Thus, as you believe and key into these anointed words, every issue in your life shall fizzle out in Jesus' Name. Amen!*

Prayer: *I believe in this prophecy. Thus, every reproach in my life is removed now in Jesus' Name. Amen!*

October 16th

[1st Corinthians 3:20] *"And again, "The Lord knows the thoughts of the wise, that they are <u>futile.</u>"*
FUTILE [GREEK]: *"MATAIOS"*

The Greek word for *'futile'* is *"Mataios"* as used in the above text-verse and in: **[1st Corinthians 15:17; Titus 3:9 and James 1:26]** Strong Concordance #3152: This word means *"pointless"* and *"purposeless."*
The New Testament writers, especially Paul, used it to depict the meaninglessness that pervades fallen human beings' thought life. Paul characterizes the *"thought of the wise"* as futile **[1st Corinthians 3:20],** and he describes the Gentiles as living *"in the futility of their minds, having their understanding darkened"* because they are *"alienated from the life of God"* **[Ephesians 4:17-18].**
The unregenerate idea is futile and aimless because they lack divine insight; they produce a life of purposelessness and ineffectiveness. Salvation from such futility comes from the indwelling Spirit of Christ in believers **[Romans 8:10-11 and Romans 8:26-27].**

Prayer: *Holy Spirit, regenerate my ideas and thoughts with your fire in Jesus' Name. Amen!*

Third Sunday in October

SUNDAY SCHOOL: **THE GREAT COMMISSION ACCORDING TO LUKE" Part 2 of 5**

1.   **WHAT IS PROPER REPENTANCE?** Some misconceptions of repentance are: **[a] That repentance is merely being sorry, [b] That repentance is a changed life.** Proper repentance may result in being sorry and changed, yet that alone is not adequate repentance. The concept of appropriate repentance is a complete "change of mind, and this involves both a turning from sin and a turning to God." **[James 4:7]**.

We submit to God by abandoning our selfish pride [James 4:1-6]. Submitting to the Lord also involves putting on the whole armor of God. That is placing all our trust and faith in God through Jesus Christ, immersing our all, in obeying God's Word **[Ephesians 6:10-18]**.

Secondly, we must resist Satan, the devil; by resisting any temptation, satan brings our way. We must recognize that temptation is not sin; it is falling to such temptation that is sin. If temptation is sin, it then means that Jesus sinned because He was tempted. But the good news is that He did not succumb to the temptations. There is no scripture stating that we would not be tempted. The scripture said in **[Psalm 34:19]** *"Many are the afflictions of the righteous...."* **[See Isaiah 43:2; 1ˢᵗ Corinthians 10:13]**.

Genuine repentance involves a change of mind in which we decide to turn from sin and turn to God. Thus, repentance is a decision preceded by sorrow and followed by a changed life.

True repentance involves rejecting our former attitudes and opinion concerning who Jesus Christ is and accept Him for Who and what He declares Himself to be, a declaration confirmed by His resurrection and ascension. It involves the renewal of our minds. **[Romans 12:2 AMPC].**

Paul, the Apostle, when he was Saul, was killing Christians, thinking he was fighting for God while fighting against God. He was doing what he thought is the correct course of action. But Christ's revelation changed his thought. Without the revelation of Christ, our thinking cannot change. And if our thought pattern is not changed, our repentance cannot be genuine.
Paul's teaching and preaching of the gospel became the proof that he has changed, that his repentance was genuine. Genuine repentance is evidenced by changed behavior.

In, **[Zechariah 1:3]** The term *'Return to Me'* reminds us of God's unconditional love. God is Love. **[See Jeremiah 3:22; 1ˢᵗ John 4:8; 1ˢᵗ John 4:16; 1 John 4:19; John 3:16].**
In our next lesson, we shall learn how genuine repentance is produced.

Prayer: *Holy Spirit! Help me change my thoughts as I turn away from sin and unto you in Jesus' Name!*

October 18th

"...... [physical and mental strength and ability] over all the power that the enemy [possesses]; and nothing shall in any way harm you." **[Luke 10:19 AMPC]**

NO MORE HURT

I had always wondered why despite the promise of God all over the Bible, many Believers still melt with fear when faced with challenges such as afflictions, satanic and demonic attacks, etc. until I arrived at a straightforward conclusion IGNORANCE! **[Hosea 4:6]** *says, "my people are destroyed for lack of knowledge: because thou hast rejected knowledge...."*From experience, I learned that the more you know about your right, the more likely you can appropriate it. You cannot be what you do not know. It is your understanding of God's Word that will make you stand out in life. Say, for an instant, though it is the right of a three-year-old daughter to eat whatever she desires in her father's house, the housemaid could withhold food from her for as long as she [the maid] desires. On the other hand, this is not likely to happen when the child becomes thirty-three years old. Right! So is the case of a Believer, who is ignorant of God's promises; he is like a three-year-old babe. He/she is susceptible to all kinds of satanic threats and afflictions. He/she is subject to the whims and caprices of demonic forces and the power of darkness. *Are you in that category? This day, I come to de-categorize you! Have the world system put you in a compartment? Be released now by fire in Jesus' Name!*

TESTIMONY TUESDAY

"I married in 2010 to a man who claimed to be an engineer, but after the marriage, I realize his claims were all falsehood to lure me into marrying him; he was a witch doctor. So, I decide to opt-out of the marriage. Within six months, we were divorced; in anger, my ex-husband cursed and cast a spell on me, and for the following nine years, I was afflicted with all manner of diseases that defied sciences, and no one could explain my ordeal. I went from hospital to hospital, from one prayer house to another, one church to another in desperation, seeking a cure.

Then I learned of THE ORACLE PRAYER CONFERENCE LINE and came on: Apostle Stevie prayed for me and placed me on a seven-day fast. On the fifth day, everything changed. I became whole again. And I called the man of God and told him I am well now can I stop the fasting, because I have never previously fasted beyond three days, he prayed and said if I want to know who was responsible for my ordeal, I should continue with the fast and that the person will not only confess, but he will carry his evil load and in ninety days I will be married. So, I continued with the fast. On the seventh day of my fast, a strange thing occurred. My ex- came to confess that he was responsible for my affliction, and a few days later, he became afflicted with every ailment I went through. I give God all the glory for saving my life. Now I am married and expecting a set of twins, a boy, and a girl, to God be the glory! Sister Irena J. Concord, NC.

DEEP DIGGING: **THE GREAT COMMISSION ACCORDING TO LUKE" Part 3 of 5**

HOW IS GENUINE REPENTANCE PRODUCED?
Repentance is produced by godly sorrow [2nd Corinthians 7:9-10]. Real sorrow leads to genuine repentance, but sadness is not repentance. **It is godly sorrow that leads to true repentance,** not worldly sorrow: **2nd Corinthians 7:10].**
Unlike godly sorrow, the kind of sorrow and remorse the worldly and ungodly experience leads to suicide and produces death. Remember Judas Iscariot in **[Matthew 27:3-7].** But in the case of Peter's denial of Jesus, he turned to God and fulfilled his destiny because his repentance was genuine. Godly sorrow for sins leads to a change of mind and a turning to God. Because repentance means turning to God after a change of mind, who is the Savior, therefore, there can be no deliverance without repentance, whether physical or spiritual deliverance, which is salvation. **[2nd Corinthians 6:2, Obadiah 1:17].**

Godly sorrow is that which is directed toward God because one has sinned against a holy, and loving God, not because one got 'caught' [notice David's attitude] in **[Psalm 51:4]** Remember Joseph in **[Genesis 39:9b].**
ADAM AND EVE: [Genesis 3]. The right kind of sorrow produces the proper change of mind, leading to salvation:

ONE YEAR BIBLE PLAN: Jer 33-34/ Philipp. 2:1-30

"For God is not the author of confusion but peace, as in all the churches of the saints." **[1st Corinthians 14:33]**

REFUSE TO BE CONFUSE

Confusion is not from God: it is one of Satan's tools of distraction. When we try too hard to figure things out in our minds instead of trusting God, we get confused. He always offers us peace, not confusion. If you are confused, know that something is not right, and it is time to turn to God for help.

Maybe you have been trying to solve your problems in your strength and wisdom without Jesus. Thankfully, He is ready and willing to help, so you can surrender the struggle and entrust yourself totally to Him. He has got your back.

Once you turn from your efforts and reason to God's grace, you open a door for Him to show you what you need to know to handle whatever problem or situation you face. As you learn to rest in Him, you will find the divine rest and direction you desire.

Prayer: *Father, thank You for giving me peace instead of confusion. Help me to live in Your grace, knowing that You can handle whatever situation or circumstance I may face. Thank You for Your peace; I choose to receive it now in abundance Jesus' Name. Amen!*

ONE YEAR BIBLE PLAN: JER 35-36/ PHILIPP. 3:1-21

"Cast not away, therefore, your confidence, which hath great recompense of reward." **[Hebrews 10:35]**

CONFIDE IN CHRIST JESUS

[Hebrews 10:35-39]; Losing trust in Christ's ability to do anything has profound implications. If you lose confidence in the all-sufficiency of Jesus Christ's atonement for your sin, you quickly turn to idols for supplementary atonement. Paul wrote to the Galatians: *"I do not frustrate the grace of God: for if righteousness come by the law, then Christ is dead in vain"* **[Galatians 2:21].** The Galatians had lost confidence in the grace that earned them salvation and resorted to self-righteousness through religious activities.

Today, like the Galatians, many do not think that the gospel is enough for them. So, they give in to satanic options. **[Galatians 3:1; Galatians 3:3].** Do not lose confidence in God due to impatience. The just shall live by faith **[Romans 1:17].** Do not blaspheme because things are not going as planned. Jesus Christ is the same yesterday, today, and forever **[Hebrews 13:8].** Nothing should make you fret. God wants you to trust Him completely; there is no problem He cannot resolve. Never seek solutions to your problems from the devil or his agents. **[Psalms 16:4].** Make God your refuge and strength. He is the very present help and will never forsake you **[Psalms 46:11, Romans 8:35].**

October 23rd

WORD OF THE ORACLE

[1st Corinthians 3:16] *"Do you not know that you are the **temple** of God and that the Spirit of God dwells in you?"*

TEMPLE [GREEK]: *"NAOS"*

The Greek word for *'Temple'* is *"Naos"* as used in the above text-verse and **[1st Corinthians 6:19; 2nd Corinthians 6:16; Ephesians 2:21 and Revelation 21:22]** Strong Concordance #:3485.

This Greek word for temple refers more to the building itself, *'hieron,'* which was used to indicate the entire temple complex.

Paul told the believers that each of their bodies was a *'naos,'* a sanctuary for God **[1st Corinthians 6:19]**. As Christ's Body, Paul also said that the church is a spiritual temple for God **[1st Corinthians 3:16-17; 2nd Corinthians 6:16 and Ephesians 2:21]**.

What an extraordinary privilege it is to be God's spiritual dwelling place, both individually and corporately. The glory of God filled the tabernacle in **[Exodus 40:34]**, and the temple in **[1st Kings 8:10-11]** and thus inhabits the entire church.

There will be no need for a physical temple in the New Jerusalem because God and the Lamb will be the eternal temple **[Revelation 21:22]**.

ONE YEAR BIBLE PLAN: Jer. 39-40/ Col. 1:1-29

SUNDAY SCHOOL
THE GREAT COMMISSION

ACCORDING TO LUKE" Part 4 of 5
HOW TRUE REPENTANCE MANIFESTS?

True repentance manifests in a changed life **[2ⁿᵈ Corinthians 7:11; Ephesians 5:16 NASB]**. Redeeming the time is taking advantage of service opportunities. We all have a limited amount of time on earth, and we have all waste so much time in sin and the evil world, so we must use as much of our time for kingdom work, winning souls, being diligence, in the clearing of ourselves of self, indignation, and fear.

True repentance produces works and deeds befitting repentance **[Acts 26:20]**. Such as confessing Jesus and being baptized into Christ, baptism by immersion: **PHILIP AND THE ETHIOPIAN EUNUCH: [Acts 8:36-38]**. The eunuch, having heard the gospel, responded to the conviction of the Holy Spirit. The eunuch went home and became a missionary in Ethiopia. Such is walking in the works that God has ordained for one in Christ **[Ephesians 2:10]**. Apathy, halfhearted service, Lukewarmness, and slothfulness do not indicate true repentance! **[Revelation 3:15-16]**. Often, those who repented when they first came to Christ need to repent again **[Revelation 2:4-5]**. *Wherever there is true repentance, remission of sins follows.* In our next lesson, we shall learn: ***WHAT REMISSION OF SIN IS?***

October 25th

"You have your life through Christ, Jesus. He showed us God's plan of salvation; he was the one who made us acceptable to God..." **[1st Corinthians 1:30 TLB]**

MATCHLESS JESUS

More and more, I am becoming aware of the truth that people change people as much as ideas change people. The power of personality is vital. One could find many illustrations to prove that personality is often more significant than ideas. Such is the case with Christianity.

The secret of the power of Christianity is not in its ethics. It is not in Christian ideas or philosophy, although Christianity has a philosophical set of ideas. The secret of Christianity is found in a Person, and that Person is the Lord Jesus Christ.

Men have discovered other philosophical and ethical systems, but they have not found another Jesus Christ. No one in history can match Christ. So, hold on to the personality of Christ and His love, and you shall acquire hour heart's desire in due season.

Prayer: *Lord, as I tell others of Your love, help me to hide my personality in Yours, in Jesus' Name.*

TESTIMONY TUESDAY

ONE YEAR BIBLE PLAN: Jer. 43-44/ Colossians 3:1-2
[John 3:16-17] *"For God so loved the world, that he gave his only begotten Son, that whosoever believeth in him should not perish, but have everlasting life. For God sent not his Son into the world to condemn the world; but that the world through him might be saved."*

I NO LONGER DESIRE TO DIE

Here is Michelle's testimony:
During the end of 2016 and the early part of 2017, I suffered from a terrible depression that led me to start thinking about committing suicide. Around about that time, I was talking to some people on a few forums about my problems. One of those people helped me learn a little bit about Jesus. And introduced me to the Oracle of Int'l Ministries online. I also found out about prayer on the internet, which led me to read about Jesus. Eventually, I realized that even the person who had helped me learn about Jesus could not help me. It seemed like the only one who could help me was the Lord himself.
I felt like I could not trust people, so I turned to the Lord. Now I am doing a lot better, and I am no longer suicidal. I trust people more, and the Lord has changed me so much! Thanks to Jesus, I no longer want to die! If it were not for him, I do not think I would have made it. That is not all he has done, though; He has saved me so I could have everlasting life! Sister M.

WEDNESDAY, October 27th

DEEP DIGGING: **THE GREAT COMMISSION ACCORDING TO LUKE" Part 5 of 5 WHAT IS REMISSION OF SINS?**

The word remission means "to remit" and involves a dismissal, a release. A key synonym often used in some translations is the word "forgiveness" Other terms and metaphors used in the Bible to describe "remission" of sins include:

    a. Sins are **"taken away"** – **[John 1:29; Romans 11:27]**

    b. Sins are **"blotted out"** – [Acts 3:19]

    c. Sins are **"washed away"** – [Acts 22:16]

    d. Sins are **"covered"** – [Romans 4:7]

    e. Sins are **"not imputed"** – [Romans 4:8]

    f. Sins are **"purged"** – [Hebrews 1:3; 2nd Peter 1:9]

    g. Sins are **"remembered no more"** – [Hebrews 8:12]

All these terms signify the removal of the guilt of sin from the sinner! And a sinner so forgiven is "justified" **[1st Corinthians 6:11]**. That is akin to a legal term, which means "not guilty."

PROPERLY REMISSION OF SINS

Remission of sins is made possible through the Blood of Jesus Christ! **[Matthew 26:28].** The alien sinner [one who is not yet a Christian] receive proper remission of sin by:

a. Believing [trusting] in Jesus – [Acts 10:42-43]
b. By repenting and being baptized – [Acts 2:38]

The erring Christian who sins after they have been baptized receive remission of sin by:

c. Repenting and praying [Acts 8:22]
d. By confessing one's sins to God [1st John 1:9]

Note that in both cases, remission of sins is tied to repentance! And when a person recognizes who Jesus is, the result is usually a desire to do what He commands. So, after repentance and remission of sins, Baptism follows the first action required of a new believer. **[Matthew 28:19-20]**

CONCLUSION: *Do you desire the blessing of having your sins remitted?*
It is only possible through the Blood of Jesus! It requires true repentance brought about through godly sorrow for your sins.
 Are you willing to do "works befitting repentance"?
Not works done to earn or merit the remission of sins. But acts of faith done to receive God's grace and mercy through the Blood of Christ. If you are a sinner still outside of Christ, then believe in Jesus, repent of sins, confess Jesus, and be baptized for the remission of yours.
If you are an erring Christian, then repent of your sins and pray, knowing that God will cleanse you of all unrighteousness!

"........ favored and to be envied is she who believed that there would be a fulfillment of the things that were spoken to her from the Lord." **[Luke 1:45 AMPC]**

BELIEVE TO RECEIVE

God does not speak empty words. He is an action God, so whatever He says, He does. He is not a man that He should lie. However, the onus is on us to receive God's promises accordingly by believing, claiming what we believe, and pray.

Many delay God's promises by doubting and weakens God's hand by so doing. In **[Matthew 13:54-58]**, Jesus could not perform any major miracles in Nazareth because they did not believe Him; the word did not work for them. That is why **[Luke 1:45]** says, *"Blessed is she that believed..."*

Has God promised you anything through dreams and visions? Have His prophets declared His Word over you? Have you caught a Rhema in God's Word?

Beloved, believe in the Lord and the power of His might, and God shall perform those things He has promised you in Jesus' Name. Amen!

Prayer: *My Lord and My God! I believe that you can* **[Affix the promise].** *Fulfill these promises for me in Jesus' Name. Amen!*

<h1 style="text-align:center">October 29th</h1>

"...And the waters returned and covered the chariots, and the horsemen, and all the host of Pharaoh..." **[Exodus 14:28]**

SINKING PURSUERERS!

After the Lord had slain the first-born sons of Egypt, Pharaoh was forced to free Israel from captivity **[Exodus 12:29-42].** However, as soon as they left, Pharaoh and his host pursued them intending to destroy the Israelites. Soon Israel came to the red sea, and then Moses stretched out his hand as directed by God, and the Red Sea parted. **[Exodus 14:21-28].**

Considering Pharaoh's ordeal thus far with all the plagues and the parting of the Red Sea, one would expect; Pharaoh would stop the pursuit for fear of the God of Israel. But no! He continued because he was a very stubborn enemy. He did not stop until he was buried in the Red Sea' with all his warriors.

Today, Pharaoh and his soldiers' may be history, but such stubborn enemies still abound. Some of them may have been pursuing your family even before you were born. Such powers must give way for you to get on with your destiny. *I decree every stubborn pursuer of your future is buried in the Red Sea in the Name of Jesus. As you believe and claim this prophecy, those evil forces pursuing you shall collapse and never rise again in Jesus' Name. Amen!*

Prayer: *Enemies pursuing me, drown in Jesus' Name!*

October 30th

WORD OF THE ORACLE

[1st Corinthians 8:9] *"But beware lest somehow this **liberty** of yours become a stumbling block to those who are weak."*

LIBERTY [GREEK]: ***"EXOUSIA"***

The Greek word for *'liberty'* is ***"Esousia"*** as used in the above text-verse and **[1st Corinthians 9:18; Matthew 7:29 and Romans 9:21]** Strong Concordance #:1849.

The Greek term usually denotes *"right,"* *"authority,"* or even *"privilege."* In specific contexts, like this one, it connotes the freedom to exercise right. Specifically, Paul addressed the Corinthians' right to eat meat that may have come from pagan temples. The eating of sacrificial food, the cultic meals in pagan temples, was criticized by Paul because it was understood that participants in those meals were uniting themselves to demons **[1st Corinthians 10:19-21].**

However, Paul had no problem with purchased food leftover from those events and sold in the marketplace. In his judgment, if they ate it at home, they were not participating in idolatry. They had the liberty or right to eat this food with a good conscience. The exception was if, by so doing, they would destroy the faith of a weaker believer. For the sake of such believers, one should abstain.

Fifth Sunday in October

SUNDAY SCHOOL: **THE GREATEST NEED Part 1 of 4**

Many are the needs of our day and age. There is a need for peace in war-torn nations. There is a need for food and clothing in poverty-stricken nations. There is a need for loving families, civil rights, good-paying jobs. All these needs are undoubtedly noble and especially important, yet the greatest need for our world today is evangelism: That is: Sharing the gospel with every person **[Mark 16:15]**.

Evangelism, which is preaching and reaching out to the world with the gospel, is the greatest need of our time. **[Acts 8:5]**.

Outreaching with the gospel of grace is a need that was met aggressively in the first century AD **[Colossians 1:23]**.

But the reason why evangelism is "The Greatest Need" may not be apparent to some, so the reminder is vital:

Thus: *in our next lesson, we shall study why the need is so great.*

November 1st

PRAISE GOD

"I will bless the Lord at all times; His praise shall continually be in my mouth……." **[Psalm 34:1-3 AMPC]**

David said, *"I will bless the Lord at all times; His praise shall continually be in my mouth."* Then God said, "In that case, David, your kingdoms shall be established forever." *As your praise ascends unto God today, your greatness shall never descend in the Name of Jesus Christ. Amen!*

PRAISE THE LORD NOW:

Lord, you are The Alpha and The Omega; The Beginning and The Ending, The One who was, The One who is, and The One who will ever be! The Unchangeable Lord! My Redeemer! The Great Physician! Wonderful! Counselor! Mighty God! The Prince of Peace! The everlasting Father, The Rock of Ages. I Bless Your Holy Name in Jesus' Name, I worship. Amen!

BIRTHDAY AND ANNIVERSARY PRAYERS

Father, I commit all your November children and those celebrating an anniversary this month unto you. Lord, as they begin a New Year in their lives, everything that is old, replace it with something new. Give them new joy, new blessings, breakthroughs. In all areas of their lives, let everything become new and let them serve you to the very end, in Jesus' Name!

TESTIMONY TUESDAY

"……. For all the land which thou seest, to thee will I give it, and to thy seed forever." **[Genesis 13:14-18]**

DIVINE INSPIRATION

There is a considerable difference between a divinely inspired person and a person motivated by success. Whereas the latter requires a great deal of human effort to get just little results, the former requires just a little human effort to produce great results. The Presiding Bishop of The Living Faith Church, David Oyedepo, said, *"Years ago, I was walking around the premises of Oral Roberts University in the USA, and looking at the fantastic structures, I told myself, 'it can happen anywhere.' That was on about five hundred acres of land. Today, by the grace of God, our ministry has over seven hundred acres of land."* Bishop Oyedepo said this while trying to explain the power that inspired the building of one of the world's greatest masterpieces, of the living faith church.

The Bishop was not the only one that had walked Oral Roberts University. But whereas others enjoy the magnificence of the edifice, others wondered aloud at the university's sheer splendor, but the Bishop was inspired to build something greater in Africa. What are the good things you see around? Do you simply admire the work of others? Begin to think creatively today. As you do, I prophesy you shall be divinely inspired to achieve tremendous success in Jesus' Name.

WEDNESDAY, November 3rd

DEEP DIGGING: **THE GREATEST NEED Part 2 of 4**
WHY IS THE NEED SO GREAT?
1. THE CONDITION OF THE WORLD: *What is the condition of the world?* Billions are dying, lost in their sin: **[Romans 3:23].** Without Christ, the Object and Subject of the gospel, they will die in their sins **[John 8:24].** That means we all have relatives, friends, and neighbors that would be lost. And we are doing little or nothing to reach out to them.

In many nations, souls die and will yet die outside of Christ because many Believers are unwilling to go or be sent to reach out to them. **[Romans 10:14-15].** So, unless we do something to meet this need, even more souls will be lost!

THE NEED IS SO GREAT *Because of:*
THE CONDITION OF THE CHURCH: Many congregations have lost their focus: Church Assemblies have become little more than social clubs: Meeting only the members' social and emotional needs. Churches have become over-burdened by that which is the responsibility of other social and governmental institutions **[1st Timothy 5:16].**

Congregations are declining instead of increasing as Christians die or fall away, and little is being done to convert others:

And where there is numerical growth, it is due to Christians moving into the areas; some are just moving from one church assembly to the other, no new coverts whatsoever. And unless we do something to meet this need, many churches will cease to exist in no time! So, to save others and save ourselves, we need to evangelize!

WHY THE NEED IS NOT BEING MET

1. A LACK OF CONCERN: Many believers are not concerned about the Lord's cause, who came to seek and save us **[Luke 19:10]**. We are not concerned for those that are lost and dying in sin, unlike Paul **[Romans 10:1]**. We are not concerned for our spiritual welfare and wellbeing, endangered by failing to bear fruit **[John 15:1-2]**. We have become so hardened that we no longer care.

#2. FOR SOME, IT IS A LACK OF KNOWLEDGE:

[a] Lacking knowledge of God's Word: Many are unaware that Jesus commissioned us to this mission **[Matthew 28:19; Mark 16:15; 1ˢᵗ Peter 2:9]**. *Perhaps many need to be taught again so we may teach others* **[Hebrews 5:12 AMPC]**.

[b] Lacking knowledge of what to do, and what to say: When it can often be as simple as saying, "Come and see" **[John 1:45-46]**. When it involves merely sharing with others what you believe:

Are we willing to try to learn that others might be saved?

November 4th

"Above all, love each other deeply, because love covers..." **[1st Peter 4:8 NIV]**

ABOVE ALL!

People often try to make others fit into their mold, conform to their ideas, and be just like them. We think, *"If they changed, I wouldn't get upset. If they did it the way I want, they wouldn't get on my nerves."* But really, we need to give people room to be who God created them to be. Life is too short to spend it trying to fix everybody. Sure, we should encourage people and help them grow and come up higher. But we must get to the point where we step back and say, *"All right, this is who God made them be, and I'm going to accept them the way they are. Just because they do not have my same strengths, I'm not going to let that frustrate me."*

We must choose to love everyone because love covers our differences and offenses. Love makes allowances for other people's weaknesses. Love overlooks a wrong done to it. Love allows us to appreciate what others bring into our lives, and it brings us together in unity. Today, above all, choose love. Choose to focus on the things that make your relationships more robust because, in the end, love is all that remains.

Prayer: *Lord, I choose to set my heart and mind on You. I choose to love others the way You have commanded. Give me the strength to walk in Your ways in Jesus' Name. Amen!*

November 5th

[Matthew 7:11] *"...how much more will your Father who is in heaven give good things to those who ask him!"* **GOOD THINGS!**

The word "Good" means *"useful; valuable; having qualities or a tendency to produce a beneficial effect."* God is good, without respect to persons. In other words, He is useful to all, all the time. Goodness radiates from Him.

Not everything in life is good, but God can work it out for good if we trust Him. Joseph suffered much abuse at the hands of his brothers as a youth, but later in life, when he had an opportunity to get revenge against them, he said: *"...you thought evil against me, but God meant it for good..."* **[Genesis 50:20].** Joseph could have been bitter, but he searched for the good in his painful situation.

God's motive and purpose are to do good to everyone who will receive it from Him. God is always good because it is His trait. God is unlike humans because His ways and thoughts are far above ours **[Isaiah 55:8–9].**

Prayer: *Father, thank You for being so good all the time. Help me to trust in Your goodness throughout my days in Jesus' Name. Amen!*

November 6th

WORD OF THE ORACLE

[1st Corinthians 10:14] *"Therefore, my beloved, flee from __idolatry.__"*

IDOLATRY [GREEK]: ***"EIDOLOLATREIA"***

The Greek word for *'Idolatry'* is ***"Eidoloatreia"*** as used in the above text-verse and in: **[Galatians 3:20 and Colossians 3:5]** Strong Concordance #1495:

This word refers to the practice of worshipping idols. Related to this, Greek word is translated *"idolater"* in **[1st Corinthians 5:10-11; 1st Corinthians 10:7]; idol"** in **1st Corinthians 8:4, 1st Corinthians 8:7, 1st Corinthians 10:19, 1st Corinthians 12:2]; and "things offered to idols" in 1st Corinthians 8:1 and 1st Corinthians 10:28].**

The fullest discussion in the New Testament concerning idolatry is in First Corinthians. Paul had told the Corinthians not to associate with those who called themselves believers but were still idolaters **[1st Corinthians 5:9-11].**

The Corinthians must have asked Paul for clarification on this matter, for in First Corinthians, Paul warns the believers to refrain from all forms of idol worship.

Prayer: *Lord crushes out every spirit of idolatry in my life in the Name of Jesus Christ. Amen!*

First Sunday in November

SUNDAY SCHOOL: **THE GREATEST NEED Part 3 of 4**
WHY THE NEED IS NOT BEING MET
3. FOR SOME, IT IS A LACK OF COURAGE:
  i.   **There is a fear of being:** *#1. Reject by loved ones; #2 Fear of being ridiculed by friends and strangers #3 and reviled by enemies of Christ.*
  ii.   **Yet there is no need to fear such things:** #1. People are not rejecting us, but Christ, #2. If reviled for the Name of Christ, we are blessed **[Matthew 5:11-12; 1st Peter 4:14-16].**
  iii.   **If we are servants of Christ, we seek to please God, not man [Galatians 1:10].**

4. FOR SOME, IT IS A LACK OF FAITH: Those who do not believe that God's Word is true: Even when it describes the world's sinful condition **[Romans 3:23]**, even when it describes the terrible consequences of sin **[Romans 6:23; Revelation 21:8]**.
Some do not believe in the ability of God Himself: To give them the strength to do His will **[Phil. 4:13]**. To give them the wisdom to teach His Word **[James 1:5]**. To give them the courage to share His Will **[2nd Timothy 1:7-8]**. *Are we willing to have the faith to trust in God, that others might be saved?*

November 8th

"All we like sheep have gone astray; we have turned everyone to his way, and the LORD hath laid on him the iniquity of us all." **[Isaiah 53:6]**

THE WEIGHT OF SIN

Many do not understand what happened when Christ died on the Cross. At Calvary, Jesus carried the weight of our sins, and God judged Him for it. God then will not judge us because the full weight of sin is being laid on Christ. That is why He prayed, saying: *"Father, if thou be willing, remove this cup from me: nevertheless, not my will, but thine, be done."* **[Luke 22:42]**

There is no other way! It must be through the Cross for the remission of sin. And for the first time, God's eyes could not behold His only Begotten Son because of our sin. There was a separation between the Father and the Son. And Jesus said, *'My God, My God, why hast thou forsaken me?'* **[Matthew 27:46].** Notice He did not say, my Father, as usual, but my God.

Jesus had always enjoyed Abba, but this time around, Abba turned His back on His Son. He called Him My God so that we can call Him Abba Father. When you are in a tight corner, cry out to your Daddy, and your Daddy will rise and stop everyone and everything hindering you. **[Romans 8:32].** And whatever you believe God for will happen in your life. You will not be denied in Jesus' Name. **[Romans 8:26-39, 2nd Corinthians 5:11-21].**

TESTIMONY TUESDAY

[Hebrews 9:11-28], Problems are forerunners of miracles. When you have a problem, if you are a real child of God, it means that testimony is on the way. If there are no problems, how will you ever have a testimony?

Who can make you dwell in safety? Not the police nor are night guards. It is only God. **[Psalm 4:8]** If He is the One who can keep you safe, then you must hand everything over to Him. **[Psalm 29:11].** If you are one of His people, you should have your share of that peace. **[John 14:27].** It is Christ who gives true lasting peace. If you have given your life to Jesus, there is nothing to worry about. One way by which the devil can get you to worry is by telling you that you were such a wicked sinner and that you cannot escape punishment. That is the lie of the devil. Once you give your life to Jesus Christ, you are already justified. **[Romans 5:1]**

What is the secret of our peace? Why do we have peace with God? It is not because we are good. It is because we have surrendered our lives to Jesus. All our sins were forgiven the day we gave our life to Jesus. **[Ephesians 2:13-14].** Christ is our peace. No matter what you are going through now, you have assured God's peace. The peace, which Jesus gives, triumphs over the topsy-turvy conditions of life. *My prayer for you is that the peace of God will fill your heart now and always in the Name of Jesus Christ. Amen!* **[1ˢᵗ Peter 3:15]**

ONE YEAR BIBLE PLAN: **GREATEST NEED Pt 4 of 4**

WHY THE NEED IS NOT BEING MET
#5. FOR SOME, IT IS A LACK OF FOCUS:

[a] Distraction of worldly things: Stifles our efforts to bear fruit **[Luke 8:14]** *"The seed that fell among thorns stands for those who hear, but as they go on their way they are choked by life's worries, riches, and pleasures, and they do not mature."*

It makes one unprepared for the day of the Lord [Luke 21:34] *"Be careful, or your hearts will be weighed down with carousing, drunkenness and the anxieties of life, and that day will close on you suddenly like a trap."*

[b] Trying to do the impossible: Such as serving two masters **[Luke 16:13]** *"No one can serve two masters. Either you will hate the one and love the other, or you will be devoted to the one and despise the other. You cannot serve both God and money."*

[c] Such as loving both the Father and the world: [1st John 2:15-17]. And this is the primary reason why people do not evangelize today: ***Are you willing to seek first the kingdom of God, making its growth your priority?***

There is no acceptable excuse for not meeting "The Greatest Need." ***We would learn more next week.***

   <u>Prayer:</u> *Lord, give me the grace to evangelize to lost souls.*

November 11th

"He who pursues righteousness and loyalty finds life…"
– [Proverbs 21:21 NASB]

LOYALTY

Righteousness and loyalty go together. If we are not loyal to our family, friends, job, country, we cannot experience God's best. Dedicated people are honorable people. Faithful people stick with their friends through thick and thin. When you are loyal, you keep your word.

Loyal people are respectful of their country's laws and leaders. Trustworthy people honor their parents and defend their families. When you are faithful, you are a person of integrity. You build trust with others. It is where you can rise higher.

Are you faithful in the things you do? Can you be more loyal? Do not let the distractions of everyday life keep you from being dedicated. Look for ways to show honor. Is there something you need to set aside for the sake of a loved one? Show love by staying loyal. As Scripture promises, you will find the abundant life that God planned for you when you pursue loyalty, honor, and righteousness!

Prayer: *Father, thank You for the promise of life in Your Word. Show me any area where I can rise pursuing loyalty. Help me to be more faithful. Let Your light shine through me as I seek righteousness and faithfulness today in Jesus' Name!*

November 12th

"…… . Where is he? And Ziba said unto the king, Behold, he is in the house of Machir, the son of Ammiel, in Lodebar. Then King David sent, and fetched him out of the house of Machir…… " **[2nd Samuel 9:1-13]**

COMING OUT

Lodebar means forsook and forgotten. It represents a ghetto and barren land. It means left behind to die. Lodebar was a place for the downtrodden, lowly, and the poor. It was no place for a prince or person of royal birth. But unfortunately, it was home for Mephibosheth, Saul's grandson, the first king of Israel. I do not know where you are on the ladder of life today. Maybe the harsh realities of life have made you a second-class citizen. Or you have now lost confidence in yourself and the world system. *Whatever is your situation, I tell you that you are coming out of the pit this day in Jesus' Name. Amen!* Mephibosheth had resigned himself to a life in Lodebar, but one day the king remembered him. *The King of Kings has remembered you this day in Jesus' Name. Amen!* You may have thought that God has forgotten you in the doldrums of life. But I tell you, not so! *Like David remembered Mephibosheth, the God of Abraham, Isaac, and Jacob has remembered you for lifting this day in the Name of Jesus Christ.* Therefore, arise and move forward, and upward for you are coming out of the pit!

Prayer: *Today, I arise and step into my glory.*

November 13th

WORD OF THE ORACLE

[1st Corinthians 12:1] *"Now concerning spiritual __gifts,__ brethren, I do not want you to be ignorant:"*

SPIRITUAL GIFTS [GREEK]: *"PNEUMATIKOS"*

The Greek term for *'spiritual'* is *"Pneumatikos"* as used in the above text-verse and in **[1st Corinthians 14:1, 1st Corinthians 14:37 and Romans 1:11].** Strong Concordance #4152.

And the word *'gift'* in Greek is *"Charisma"* as used in **[1st Corinthians 1:7, 1st Corinthians 7:7, 1st Corinthians 12:4 and 1st Timothy 4:14]** Strong Concordance #5486.

The Greek term **charisma** is closely akin to the word **Charis** which means *"grace"* or *"favor";* charisma denotes *"that which is graciously given."*

Paul used the term **charisma** synonymously with the Greek term ***"ta pneumatika,"*** which means *"the spiritual things"* because they are graciously given spiritual gifts. God gave these gifts to various churches to enliven the meetings and edify the church's believers. Each member is gifted with at least one kind of **charisma,** i.e., the gift of teaching, preaching, prophesying, healing working of miracles, discerning spirits, speaking in tongues, and interpretation of tongues or other gifts.

Second Sunday in November

SUNDAY SCHOOL
WHY WE ALL NEED TO BE PERSONAL WORKERS: Part 1 of 3

Last week we looked at why the most significant need, and why the needs of evangelism, are not met. Whatever the reason for "The Greatest Need" not being met, there is no excuse. To encourage us to meet this need today, we would consider why we must win souls.

TO FULFILL THE COMMAND OF CHRIST:

I. **Jesus commanded that disciples be made [Matthew 28:19]** *"Therefore go and make disciples of all nations, baptizing them in the name of the Father and of the Son and the Holy Spirit."*

II. **Disciples are taught to observe what He commanded [Matthew 28:19-20 NIV]** *"...and teaching them to obey everything I have commanded you...."*

III. **The Great Commission is not fulfilled until we are making disciples!**

Memory Verse: [Matthew 28:19 AMPC] *"Go then and make disciples of all the nations, baptizing them* *into the Name of the Father and the Son and the Holy Spirit."*

<u>Prayer:</u> *Holy Spirit enables me to disciple and mentor new converts in the Name of Jesus Christ. Amen!*

November 15th

"[Not in your strength] for it is God Who is all the while effectually at work in you [energizing and creating in you the power and desire], both to will and to work for His good pleasure and satisfaction and delight."
[Philippians 2:13]

TRUST GOD!

Most of us desire the good life God has planned for us without acquiring our hearts' desires. We know and always see areas in our lives that need to change. Many often set out to make a change, yet they are powerless to effect any change in any shape or form whatsoever despite their best efforts.

Trying to bring about change through your strength and plans will always result in frustration. God is waiting for you to stop trying to change what you cannot change. He is waiting for you to trust Him to change you and your situation.

If you need to change your thoughts, attitudes, and behavior, understand that you cannot do it yourself. Spend time with God and ask for His help. After all, if He cannot do it, it cannot be done. But He can. And He will if you completely trust Him!

Prayer: *Holy Spirit gives me the grace to put my trust in you!*

TESTIMONY TUESDAY

A CAR AND A WIFE

You'd better believe this: Before long, you will be sharing your testimony for the world and your world to see and glorify God:

"It is exactly a year today when the Holy Spirit led me onto your Facebook page. My life was in total shambles, and even though I am a believer and pray a lot, things were only getting worse. I was heavily in debt and still borrowing even more to survive. At the age of 45, I was single.

Indeed, I had come to the end of the road and lost all hope and faith in God because I had fasted all the fasting and prayed all the prayers, I knew but was still under serious financial problems, and my job was nothing to write home about.

After the monthly three days fasting and prayers for the month of October 2020, my case worsened. Life became more difficult for me. Some of my friends whom I introduced to your Facebook page started testifying, yet I have no testimony.

But today, as I write to you, I have two great testimonies. I took delivery of a brand-new SUV. And I have finally found my wife. My lady has agreed to my proposal, and she is ready to settle down with me. One thing I love about her is that she is very prayerful and God-fearing. God has, indeed, mesmerized me." Sean Q, Freetown SL.

WEDNESDAY, November 17th

DEEP DIGGING: **WHY WE ALL NEED TO BE PERSONAL WORKERS: Part 2 of 3**
TO SHOW OUR LOVE FOR OTHERS:

I. Love for others was the second greatest commandment of the Old Testament **[Matthew 22:39]**. *"And the second is like it: 'Love your neighbor as yourself."*

II. Love for one another is debt that can never be fully paid **[Romans 13:8 NIV]** *"Let no debt remain outstanding, except the continuing debt to love one another, for whoever loves others has fulfilled the law."*

III. We are to love even our enemies **[Matthew 5:44-45]**. *What greater love can we show than to offer others the way of salvation?*

TO BE LIKE THE EARLY CHURCH:

I. To be the Lord's Church, we must follow the pattern of congregational organization, worship, and work.

II. To be the Lord's Church, we must also demonstrate the same: Zeal for the Lord's cause and love for the lost:

III. Until we restore the spirit and soul of New Testament Christianity, *we are only a skeleton!*

We shall continue next week.

November 18th

ONE YEAR BIBLE PLAN: EZE 35-36/ HEB 10:1-39

"You know well enough how the wind blows this way and that. You hear it rustling through the trees, but you have no idea......" **[John 3:8 MSG]**

PROGRESS

Have you ever been caught in the whirlwind? If your answer is yes, then you would better appreciate the scripture above. Desert wind comes suddenly and disappears suddenly. It has no constant path or route. Sometimes you expect it to continue moving in a straight line only for it to stop. So, the movement of the wind is unpredictable. *That is precisely how your progress would be for the remaining part of this year in Jesus' Name. Amen!*

It will be so because, just like the wind, your progress will come from God. By nature, man is competitive and contentious. So, a man whose progress is in the hands of another man is in dire straits. But thank God, your progress and destiny are not in the hands of man but God's hand. *So, I prophesy nobody shall determine your advancement.* Since man cannot predict God, then your progress cannot be determined by man. So, place your hope and faith in God. Rededicate yourself to Him and depend on Him entirely. And you shall prevail in Jesus' Name.

Prayer: *Lord, I put my destiny in Your hands. I trust You wholly, and I know that it shall be well with me!*

November 19th

"For what knowest thou, O wife, whether thou shalt save thy husband? or how knowest thou, O man, whether thou shalt save thy wife?" **[1st Cor. 7:16]**

LIVING WITNESS

Some marriages are confronted with having to balance their relationship with their faith. Many hide their beliefs from their spouses because of fear. However, our primary responsibility after salvation is to get our loved ones saved. Failure to do so will make our relationship with them a thorn in the flesh. The truth is that you will either find yourself consciously or unconsciously withdrawing from them or being lured in to join them in their ungodliness.

When it comes to salvation, a person decides whether to accept Jesus. But to bring a loved one to Him requires diligence. You can pray them into giving their souls to God, and you can also feed them with God's Word. Your speech, character, and attitude of love and care can win them over faster. You are the only bible that many people read. So, if you profess to your spouse about your renewed life in Christ, your actions towards your spouse must also convince him or her of that change. With your godly trait, coupled with prayers and Words of faith, you will prevail. Therefore, do not watch your unbelieving spouse or family member perish without salvation; reach out to them today in love. Remain Blessed!

November 20th

WORD OF THE ORACLE

[**1ˢᵗ Corinthians 12:10**] *"To another the working of miracles, to another prophecy, to another discerning of spirits, to other different kinds of __tongues__, to another the interpretation of tongues."*

TONGUES [GREEK]: *"GLOSSA"*

The Greek term for *'tongue'* is *"Glossa"* as used in the above text-verse and in [**1ˢᵗ Corinthians 14:2, Verse 4-6, Verse 9, 13-14, 18, 28, Acts 2:4, Acts 10:46 and Acts 19:6**]. Strong Concordance #1100. The Greek term *"glossa"* means *"tongue"* or *"language."* When the Holy Spirit empowered the early believers on the Day of Pentecost, they were given the ability to speak in many different languages so that those visiting from all around the Roman world could hear the glories of God being uttered in their native tongue [**Acts 2:3-11**]. Cornelius's household also spoke in different languages when they were baptized in the Holy Spirit [**Acts 10:46**]. And the same happened with the new disciples from Ephesus [**Acts 19:6**]. From then on, some early church members spoke in different languages to pray to God in church meetings. When these languages were spoken in private, interpretation was not needed; when they were expressed in the discussions, Paul required explanation so that the others could understand and be edified [**1ˢᵗ Corinthians 14:2-27**].

ONE YEAR BIBLE PLAN: Ezek. 41-42 / Heb. 12:1-29

SUNDAY SCHOOL: WHY WE ALL NEED TO BE PERSONAL WORKERS: PART 3 OF 3
TERROR OF THE DAY OF THE LORD:

I.

o motivate us: **[2ⁿᵈ Corinthians 5:10-11]** *"For we must all appear before the judgment seat of Christ, so that each of us may receive what is due us for the things done while in the body, whether good or bad."*

II.

Jesus spoke much about souls being lost: **[Matthew 7:13-14; Matthew 7:21-23; Mark 16:16]**

III.

he reality of Judgment Day and souls lost should move us to the action!

BECAUSE OF THE JOY IN SAVING OTHERS:

I. There is the joy you can cause to happen in heaven – **Luke 15:7; Luke 15:10]**

II. There is the joy you will personally experience: Paul referred to his converts as his 'glory and joy' – **[1ˢᵗ Thessalonians 2:19-20]**

III. John had no greater joy than to see his children walk in truth **[3ʳᵈ John 4].** The pleasure is magnified, knowing that what you do will last for eternity! *Do we have faith? Do we have the right focus? Do we even care?*

Memory Verse: [3rd John 4] *"I have no greater joy than to hear that my children are walking in the truth."*

happy sunday

November 22nd

"My soul thirsteth for God, for the living God: when shall I come and appear before God?" **[Psalm 42:2]**

PASSION

What you get from God depends largely on your spiritual passion for Him. You must desire more and more of God. Your hunger and thirst must be on the increase daily. Many have been born again for years but are yet to read through the Bible. Some started, only to give up halfway. Do you want power from God? If your answer is yes, then you must hunger for God. It is not an option. Hunger for God is one of the greatest attributes of spiritual people. Why is it that some people can pray for three to four hours nonstop? It is because there is something inside them prompting them to do so. When a person can read the whole of Matthew's gospel at a sitting, there is something special inside the life of such a person. You cannot climb a spiritual mountain without subjecting yourself to a spiritual discipline. You cannot receive power without consecration. You must become so thirsty as to be eagerly coveting God's glory. Your soul must thirst for God and long for Him. That is the message underscored in today's scriptures. That thirst must begin today and remain in you as an unquenchable passion for being spiritually empowered.

Prayer: *Lord, let your zeal fall upon me now!*

TESTIMONY TUESDAY

"Since we started following you on Periscope in 2019, I will say God has indeed been amazing, and I testify that our life has changed completely.
My husband used to have mental problems, and doctors said he had schizophrenia. They said he needed medication every day to stay 'normal.' He would be admitted to the hospital every three months with a severe attack. I realized medicine and hospitals were not the solutions, and I started praying against this spirit using your prayer bullets. Since July 2020, he has been healed. He is now gainfully employed.
And for me, I have been blessed with many unusual contracts. I lost my job in May last year, but the Lord opened to me so many consultancy opportunities, and my pay has increased by almost 200%. The fascinating thing is that people call me and offer me opportunities of their own accord. The kind of work I do now allow me much more time with my family as I do not have to commute to the office daily. I can work from home. Our God is amazing." God bless you. J, Cape Town. SA
This praise report could be your portion if you believe. I prophesy before the end of this year; you will have multiple testimonies in every area of your life in the Name of Jesus Christ.
Prayer: *Lord, I believe, so let me receive according to my faith in the Name of Jesus Christ. Amen!*

WEDNESDAY, November 24th

DEEP DIGGING: **THE COST OF A FREE GIFT" Pt 1/4**

Perhaps you have heard it said: *"The best things in life are free!* "This is especially true when you consider that the "best" thing in life is a gift. I am talking of God's gift to all who will believe it, accept, and receive it: "Eternal life." Is truly a "gift from God" **[Romans 6:23]**. *"For the wages of sin is death, but the gift of God is eternal life in Christ Jesus our Lord."*

Although eternal life is a gift, which is free, it is free because a high cost was paid to offer this gift, and a high price is needed and must be paid to receive it!

You may wonder and say, high cost for a gift that is free? How can that be? This "paradox" can sometimes be difficult to comprehend? However, many teachings of Jesus Christ are often in "paradox," e.g., the Beatitudes in **[Matthew 5:3-6]**. Upon closer examination, such "paradoxes" are not contradictions but are expressions of critical spiritual truths!

In this new series, we shall consider how it is that a gift that is free can be so costly: Let us begin with:

THE FREE GIFT OF SALVATION

1. MANY HAVE A WRONG CONCEPT ABOUT HOW SALVATION IS OBTAINED: They think that salvation is earned by the "good works" they do.

Consider this statement by a devout Muslim: *"All my life I have obeyed the Koran and worshipped Allah faithfully. If, after death, I find that there is no paradise with which man may be comforted, as the Koran* *promises, I shall feel that I have been miserably cheated."*

Many professing Christians have a similar concept of attaining heaven, that their reward is received because of:

1. ***Their good life.***
2. ***Their generous giving of their money, resources, and time.***
3. ***Their faithful attendance at church.***

2. BUT SALVATION IS GOD'S GIFT TO UNDESERVING MEN: Offered to us while we were still sinners, ungodly, and enemies of God. **[Romans 5:6-8]** *"You see, at just the right time, when we were still powerless, Christ died for the ungodly. Very rarely will anyone die for a righteous person, though for a good person, someone might dare to die. But God demonstrates his love for us in this: While we were still sinners, Christ died for us."*

He offered His life for us not because we love God but because He loved us! **[1ˢᵗ John 4:9-10 AMPC].** And this gift is offered to all who will believe and receive it! **[Revelation 21:6; Revelation 22:17 AMPC].** Salvation, then, is offered "freely." But that does not mean it costs nothing? Not at all!

Next week we shall see that nothing in all the universe costs so much as salvation as we look at the Cost of Salvation.

ONE YEAR BIBLE PLAN: DAN 1-2 / JAMES 2:1-26
"… …He said I am the Light of the world. He who follows Me will not be walking in the dark but will have the Light, which is Life." **[John 8:12 AMPC]**

NO MORE WALK IN DARKNESS

Are you lost in the chaos and confusion of life? Are you groping in the dark, seeking a way out of the mess your life has become? Are you at a loss whose counsel you are to take to move your life to the next higher level? **[Psalm 1:1-3].** I tell you there is good news for you. *You will not tarry in the valley of darkness, for the light of God cometh upon you this day.*

Jesus is the answer you need. He not only shows you the way you should go; He shoulders the burden of all those who put their trust in Him in following the path of Life. So, no matter what you are going through right now, just look up to Him, and you will find respite. People might advise: *'Do this or that'* or *'Go here or there'* or *'Speak to such and such people!"* But the help of man is limited because man is limited to the perceptions of his five senses. He cannot offer support to another who is tired of life, disgusted, discouraged, and disillusioned with life. At such times only Jesus can help.

Are you in such a situation? Turn to Jesus; look up to Him; trust Him completely. He is the light of the world. Follow Him, and you will never walk in darkness again. God bless you!

November 26th

"And God said, let there be light: and there was light." –
[Genesis 1:3]

POWER IN THE WORD

There is power in God's Word. By it, He created the world. The Bible says Jesus wants to visit the home of a Centurion to heal his servant but was surprised when the Centurion asked Him to *"speak the Word only"* **[Matthew 8:8-10]**. Jesus spoke, and the servant was healed **[Matthew 8:13]**. That was a fulfillment of **[Psalm 107:20]**. *"He sent His word and healed them..."*

Many are searching for deliverance, yet they disregard the most potent weapon: God's Word. His Word says, *"Watch and pray, that ye enter not into temptation: the spirit indeed is willing, but the flesh is weak."* **[Matthew 26:41]**. What should we do? Obey, watch, increase our prayer time, so temptation will not sweep us away from the faith. *"For sin shall not have dominion over you: for ye are not under the law but grace."* **[Romans 6:14]**. Believe the Word, and you will be free from sin permanently.

[Philippians 4:19] says, *"But my God shall supply all your need according to his riches in glory by Christ Jesus."* If you believe, poverty shall become history in your life. If you are sick, **[1st Peter 2:24]** says *that Christ's stripes have healed us.* ***Beloved, as you believe the Word today, you will experience a positive turnaround in Jesus' Name. Amen!***

ONE YEAR BIBLE PLAN: DAN 5-6 /JAMES 5:1-20

WORD OF THE ORACLE

[1st Corinthians 15:12] *"Now if Christ is preached that He has been raised from the dead, how do some among you say that there is no **resurrection** of the dead?"*

RESURRECTION [GREEK]: *"ANATASIS"*

The Greek term for 'resurrection' is "Anatasis" as used in the above text-verse and in **[1st Corinthians 15:13, Verse 21, Verse 42, Acts 17:32, Romans 1:4 and 1st Peter 1:3]**. Strong Concordance #386. The Scripture often speaks of Christ's resurrection with the phrase literally "resurrection out of the dead ones." Like the wording in the first half of **[1st Cor. 15:12]** and other verses like **[Acts 17:31 and 1st Peter 1:3]**. When Scripture speaks of the resurrection in general, commonly, the phrase is "the resurrection of dead ones." Like the wording in the second half of **[1st Corinthians 15:12, 13 and 42]**.

In **[Romans 1:4]**, Christ's resurrection is spoken of as "resurrection of dead ones." The same terminology is used in **[1st Corinthians 15:21]**, where the Greek text reads: *"For since through a man's death came, so also through a man came the resurrection of dead persons."* It shows that Christ's resurrection included the resurrection of believers to eternal life. When He rose, many arose with Him, for they were united with Him in His resurrection **[Romans 6:4-5, Ephesians 2:6 and Colossians 3:1]**.

Fourth Sunday in November

SUNDAY SCHOOL:
THE COST OF A FREE GIFT Pt 2/4

In our last lesson, we considered how a gift could be free and at the same time costly: We learned that even though salvation is offered "freely," that does not mean it costs nothing! So, today we shall see that nothing in all the universe is as costly as salvation.

THE HIGH COST OF PROVIDING THE GIFT

Let us consider the various cost of the gift of salvation.

1. **WHAT IT COST THE FATHER– [John 3:16 AMPC Romans 8:32].** It cost the Almighty God the sacrifice of His only begotten Son to grant us the gift of salvation! He did not spare His Son to save us from our sins!
2. **WHAT IT COST THE SON [Philippians 2:5-8 AMPC].**

   a) The gift of salvation cost Jesus, the Son of God, the renunciation of glory and majesty, which He had with the Father before coming to this world.
   b) It cost Him the humiliation of servitude, even to the point of suffering and dying by crucifixion for our sins.

Memory Verse: [John 3:16] *"For God so loved the world that he gave his one and only Son, that whoever believes in him shall not perish but have eternal life."*

happy sunday

November 29th

"In peace, I will both lie down and sleep, for You, Lord, alone make me dwell in safety and confident trust."
[Psalm 4:8 AMPC]

GOD' PROTECTION

Do you face lonely hours at night because of illness or the loss of a loved one? Does the shadow of the night make the anxiety of your situation more significant than ever? Do doubts arise within you of God's ability to deliver you from the issues of life? Does fear flood your soul and rob you of your much-needed rest? Are you afraid of the arrows that flieth by day? *Beloved, hear ye the counsel of God, by His Oracle, fear not for the Lord will always protect you.*

The Bible says He who keeps Israel neither sleeps nor slumbers. If He led millions of people through the wilderness for forty long years, days, and nights, then do not you think He can protect you? Beloved, the Lord is ever faithful. He is aware of your fears, doubts, and frustrations. His loving eyes and protecting hands are always over you. So, there is no need to fear or be doubtful. He is round about you still, to make you dwell in safety. Commit your nights and days into His everlasting hands from right now, for the Lord will always protect you in Jesus' Name. God Bless you!

Prayer: *LORD, I put all my doubts and fears in your hands today. Protect me and make me dwell in your safety!*

TESTIMONY TUESDAY

ONE YEAR BIBLE PLAN: DAN 11-12 /1ST PET 3:1-22

[Job 42:10] *"And the Lord restored Job's losses when he prayed for his friends. Indeed, the Lord gave Job twice as much as he had before."*

TURNED CAPTIVITY!

The story of Job is a testament to the fact that God is omnipotent. And He sometimes allow His people to pass through difficult challenges to glorify His Name. For years, Job suffered torture and degradation in the hands of Satan. Job lost his job, wealth, health, children, and all the good life, yet he still trusted God. And when God felt that it was time, He *"turn the captivity of Job"* around and *"blessed the latter end of Job more than before...."* **[Job 42:12]**

Is your story like Job's? Have you lost everything or anything you had? Have your family, friends, and relative forsook you because of your string of troubles? Have you started querying your trust in God because of your sufferings?

Saint, what you have been passing through is just a phase. It started one day; it must end one day. *As the LORD liveth I prophesy today is that day of your testimony.* Therefore, begin to rejoice for the power of Satan over you is broken now, and *the God of Israel has set you free to prosper in Jesus' Name!*

Prayer: *I decree goodness and mercy shall follow me as the Lord turns around my captivity in Jesus' Name. Amen!*

WEDNESDAY, December 1st

DEEP DIGGING: **THE COST OF A FREE GIFT Pt 3/4**

3. **WHAT IT COST THE HOLY SPIRIT [2nd Thessalonians 2:13-14; Ephesians 4:30]**

a) All through the ages, The Holy Spirit is patiently wooing the hearts of sinful men through the gospel.

b) The Holy Spirit is suffering at the hands of men who ill-treats and grieves Him as they resist Him.

So, here we see that each Person of the triune Godhead [Trinity] has paid dearly to make the gift of salvation possible. So indeed, we can see "The High Cost Of The Free Gift of salvation."

But the "acceptance" of this gift is also costly: Let us look at the various expensive areas of accepting the gift of salvation.

THE HIGH COST OF ACCEPTING THE GIFT
IT COSTS THE DENIAL OF SELF, AND THE RENUNCIATION OF MUCH THAT MEN HOLD DEAR: Paul, who gladly paid the cost, expressed it vividly in **[Galatians 2:20; Philippians 3:7-8]**. One cannot accept Christ and His salvation on lesser terms than the complete surrender of self to Him!

THAT IS WHAT MAKES THE GOSPEL OF CHRIST "A HARD GOSPEL" FOR MANY TO ACCEPT:

Many want to accept Jesus as Savior, but not as Lord of their lives. Some even suggest that accepting Jesus as Savior and Lord are two entirely separate acts, but the two are inseparable **[Luke 2:11; Acts 2:36; Acts 10:36]**

Even religious leaders who have led people to think otherwise are beginning to see the error of their ways: The church today is paralyzed now of its supreme opportunity because we have committed the blasphemy of insisting that what is so costly for God shall come easy to us. We have not dared face the congregations with the hard gospel. No man can accept Jesus as "Savior of his soul" without accepting Him as "Lord of his life"! Jesus Himself made this clear when He warned His hearers that the cost of discipleship is high **[Luke 14:25-33].**

The Lordship of Jesus over self, life, and possessions must be acknowledged if we are to know Him as Savior! We must realize that Jesus commissioned His disciples to preach "repentance and remission of sins in His name" – **[Luke 24:47]**

There is no remission apart from repentance! And repentance involves the whole of life! – **[2nd Corinthians 7:10-11].** Not only being sorrowful from past deeds leads to repentance but zeal and fervor for the future, which affects how we will live.

Repentance is, therefore, the abandoning of our selfish way to go God's way in obedience and fellowship with Him.

December 2nd

ONE YEAR BIBLE PLAN: HOS 3-4 /1ST PET 5:1-14
"Let the peoples praise You, O God; let all the peoples praise You." **[Psalm 67:5]**

PRAISE GOD!

If God had not been on our side when the enemy rose against us, they would have swallowed us. Praise God for being your defender, your Protector, the One fighting your battles, worship Him for being your Provider! Praise Him for loving you. Express your appreciation of His love by praising Him as you have never done before! Praise and worship Him, magnify His Holy Name! Show Him that you love Him with praise.

PRAISE THE LORD!

Father, King of Glory; Ancient of Days, Unchangeable Lord from everlasting to everlasting I will adore and magnify Your Holy Name. You are the Almighty! There is no one like You! I worship and praise You! In Jesus' Name. Amen!

BIRTHDAY AND ANNIVERSARY PRAYERS

Father, I commit all your children born in this month and those celebrating an anniversary this month into your hand. As they begin a New Year in their lives, Lord answers them speedily and do something new for them. Give them new joy, new blessings, breakthroughs testimonies. In all areas of their lives, let everything become perfect in Jesus' Name. Amen!

December 3rd

GROW IN FAITH

"We are bound to thank God always for you, brethren, as it is meet, because that your faith groweth exceedingly, and the charity of every one of you all toward each other aboundeth" **[2nd Thessalonians 1:3].**

Our responsibility is to increase our measure of faith God has given us through His Word: **[Romans 10:17].** The less of God's Word you receive into your spirit, the less trust you will be able to express when you are faced with challenges. So, grow your faith by feeding on God's Word daily.

Do not stay at a low level of little faith. Little faith exhibits fear and doubt **[Matthew 8:26].** In **[Matthew 14],** Peter walked on water toward Jesus until he saw the waves and began to sink. The Bible says Jesus immediately *"...stretched forth His hand, and caught him, and said unto him, O thou of little faith, wherefore didst thou doubt?"* **[Matthew 14:31].**

CONFESSION: *The Word is living and active in me and inspires faith in me to overcome challenges and maintain my victorious life in Christ. I am born of the Word; therefore, I live by the Word. As I study and meditate on the Word, my faith is strengthened and improved, from glory to glory, and the blessings of acting on the Word are evident in my life, in Jesus' Name. Amen!*

December 4th

WORD OF THE ORACLE

[1st **Corinthians 15:45**] *"And so it is written, "The first man Adam became a living being." The last Adam became a **life-giving spirit."***

LIFE-GIVING-SPIRIT [GREEK]: *"PNEUMA ZOOPOIOUN"*

The Greek term for *'Life-Giving-Spirit'* is *"Pneuma Zoopoioun"* used in the above text-verse and in [2nd **Corinthians 3:6 and 1st Peter 3:18**]. Strong Concordance #4151, 2227.

The Greek expression denotes *"the spirit that gives life"* or *"the spirit that makes alive."* The Lord Jesus was raised from the dead because He was glorified and simultaneously became a life-giving spirit. The verse does not say Jesus became *"the Spirit"* since the Second Person of the Trinity did not become the Third Person.

Instead, he became a Spirit in the sense that His mortal existence and form were changed into immortal. He is now united with the Spirit in a glorified body. He is alive in the Spirit [1st **Peter 3:18**] to give life to all who believe. That is why Paul spoke of the Spirit of life in Christ Jesus. **[Romans 8:2].**

First Sunday in December

SUNDAY SCHOOL
THE COST OF A FREE GIFT Pt 4/4
"JUST ACCEPT CHRIST AND BE SAVED" IS THE APPEAL OF MANY: Many assume that it is a matter of "just accepting" Him, "with no strings attached"; however, consider the words of Jesus in **[John 14:21-23]**. To "receive Jesus," then, requires a full surrender to the Lordship of Christ, a sincere acceptance of His commandments **[John 15:10]**

That is why the "gift" of salvation still comes at a high cost of obedience of faith while offered freely. Salvation cannot be earned, nor merited, by any number of good deeds, for even after a lifetime of diligent obedience, we are still "unworthy servants" **[Luke 17:10].** It demands a full surrender to Him **[Matt. 28:18-20]**

The gift of salvation is costly because:

1. It cost God more than heaven can declare.
2. It cost Jesus the agony and shameful death of the Cross.
3. It costs the Holy Spirit, who seeks to woo us.
4.And it costs everyone who indeed receives it the total submission of self to the rightful claims of Jesus on the lives and souls of all who would be His for now and eternity! ***God the Father, The Holy Spirit, and Jesus Christ paid the high cost to offer you the gift of salvation; have you paid the high cost of accepting it? –*** **[Acts 2:36-39]**

"

December 6th

LITTLE FAITH

"Immediately, Jesus reached out his hand and caught him. "You of little faith," he said, "why did you doubt?" **[Matthew 14:31]**

Little faith is sensual faith given to reasoning. In **[Matthew 16:6],** Jesus said to His disciples, *"...Take heed and beware of the leaven of the Pharisees and the Sadducees."* They reasoned among themselves, saying, *"It is because we have taken no bread."* **[Matthew 16:7].** They did not understand what Jesus was teaching and thought He meant physical loaves of bread. Jesus perceived their carnal reasoning and said to them, *"...O ye of little faith, why reason ye among yourselves because ye have brought no bread?"* **[Matthew 16:8].** When the one with little faith feels discomfort in the stomach, he is quick to say, "I think it's because of something I ate or something I drank." Yet Jesus said, *"...and if they drink any deadly thing, it shall not hurt them..."* **[Mark 16:18].** God wants your faith to be stalwart, not weak, and not little. Therefore, study and do the Word of God; that is how to grow your faith to be healthy. Be like the Thessalonica, whose faith grew exceedingly, and those in Faith's hall of fame in **[Hebrews 11]** who used their faith for exploits.

CONFESSION: *As I study and meditate on the Word, my faith is strengthened and improved, from glory to glory.*

TESTIMONY TUESDAY

NINETY DAYS IN THE ORACLE

Praise the Lord God Almighty of the Oracle. Our God is indeed the God of Elijah and Elisha, who answers prayer by fire! And indeed, in my life and my household, God has proved Himself mighty through the ministry of Oracle Stevie Okauru.

Apostle Okauru may God continue to bless you as you win souls for him. The first 90 days of my connecting to your ministry have been a huge blessing for my family and me. Words are inadequate to express all that the Lord has done for us. All we can say is Thank You, Jesus, for the abundance in our home and lives. We now live a debt-free life!

To Cap, it all, my 19 years old son gave his life to Christ, listening to the replay of your conference on YouTube. Please join me in prayers for him to keep on the right path. May God be praised. Jesus is Lord forever, Amen!

Brother James and Sister Janet, Guyana.

WEDNESDAY, December 8th

DEEP DIGGING: **LISTENING Part 1 of 7**

During His earthly ministry, Jesus often concluded a lesson by crying out, *"He who has ears to hear, let him hear!"* For example, concerning John the Baptist in **[Matthew 11:15]** also, after the parable of the sower in **[Matthew 13:9]** and after explaining the parable of the tares in **[Matthew 13:43]**. In His letters to the churches of Asia, in **[Revelation 2:7-29 and Revelation 3:6-22]** Jesus concludes each with a similar saying: *"He who has an ear let him hear what the Spirit says to the churches."*

1. But what is the point of these sayings?

a) It is akin to saying, "What is being said is very important, so you had better pay attention and listen!" **[Mark 4:23-25 AMPC]**

b) It illustrates that Jesus had a problem that often exists today: Many people simply do not listen, or they do not listen to understand; they just hear without listening to understand. I am convinced that many today do not appreciate the importance of listening well. Since this issue of not listening concerned Jesus in His days, I think it is appropriate to ask, **"How Well Do We Listen?"** *We would answer this question in our next lesson.*

Prayer: *"Holy Spirit, give me a listening heart and ear in the Name of Jesus Christ. Amen!*

December 9th

NOT IMPOSSIBLE FOR GOD

".... You made the heavens and the earth by Your great power and by Your outstretched arm! There is nothing too hard or too wonderful...." **[Jeremiah 32:17 AMPC]**
I have met people who think and say God cannot solve their problems. There is one who said he believed that his situation was too difficult for God to solve. Nevertheless, he wrote a letter to give God the last chance to redeem His [God's] Name by solving this problem, which was enduring joblessness. I prayed for him, and he got a job within 48 hours. Today, he is living a good life. *This shall be your lot in Jesus' Name. Amen!*
Beloved, is your problem seeming to defy God? Are you in the category of those who consider their issues too big for God? Are you on the verge of losing hope and contemplating suicide? I tell you fear not for your problem is not too hard for God. God is all-powerful. He created the heavens and the earth; so, nothing is too complicated for Him.
That problem you are facing now is a minute thing with God. He can provide a job you with job the next moment. He can improve your life in an instant. Whatever you desire, have faith in God; your problem is not too hard for Him. He said I am the God of all flesh, is anything too hard for me: *I prophesy your heart desire will not be hard for God in Jesus' Name. Amen!*

<h1 style="text-align:center">December 10th</h1>

ONE YEAR BIBLE PLAN: AMOS 3-4/2 JOHN 1:1-13.

[Judges 2:16 NIV] *"Then the LORD rose judges, who saved them out of the hands of these raiders."*

LIFTED!

In life, there would always be challenges: Trials, tribulations. **[Job 14:1]** says, *"Mortals, born of woman, are of few days and full of trouble."* Indeed, life always throws challenges at you to raise you. Today's scripture supports that theory. Each time the Jews disobeyed God, He ensured that they are kept in bondage **[Judges 2:11-16]**. Nevertheless, at the fullness of time, God always raises men [Judges] to deliver Israel.

You become more significant than others when God decides to use you for such deliverance. Jephthah, Ehud, Samson, Gideon, and Deborah became great because God used them in such a capacity.

Do you desire to be used by God to solve and deliver people from their problems? Just position yourself to be used to do so. And you must change your mindset from impossibility to everything is possible. Begin to think of solutions instead of dwelling on the issues. Know also that difficulties are the processors of solutions. *And you will become a problem solver in Jesus' Name. Amen!*

Prayer: *Lord, use me to solve problems that are around me in Jesus' Name. Amen!*

ONE YEAR BIBLE PLAN: AMOS 5-6/3 JOHN 1:1-14

WORD OF THE ORACLE

[2nd Corinthians 1:22] *"Who also has **sealed** us and given us the Spirit in our hearts as a **guarantee.**"*
SEALED; GUARANTEE [GREEK]: *"SPHRAGIZO; ARRABON"*

The Greek term for *'Sealed'* is *"Sphragizo,"* as used in the above and in **[Ephesians 1:13 and Ephesians 4:30].** Strong Concordance #4972. And the Greek term for *'Guarantee'* is *"Arrabon"* as used in **[2nd Cor. 1:22; 2nd Cor. 5:5 and Ephesians 1:14].** Strong Concordance #728. The Greek word translated sealed here was a technical word denoting a seller's guarantee of the purchase's validity. As such, God's gift of the Holy Spirit is our guarantee. People commonly branded or marked personal possessions in the ancient world as they sealed letters, with a seal identifying the sender. In this passage, Paul describes believers being marked as God's possession, are ultimately redeemed **[Ephesians 1:13-14; Eph. 4:30].** Paul often used another term with sealed, namely *"Arrabon,"* translated guarantee. This Greek term was commonly used for a promissory first installment that guarantees full, final payment. Ancients also used the word to refer to an engagement ring. As Christians, we have received the Spirit as a first installment, guarantee, and foretaste of the full inheritance yet to be given **[Ephesians 1:13-14].**

SUNDAY SCHOOL
LISTENING Part 2 of 7
HOW WELL DO WE LISTEN?

**THERE ARE THREE TYPES OF LISTENERS
ACCORDING TO SCRIPTURES:**

I. **THE "DULL OF HEARING":** Some of the Hebrew Christians were like such listeners: **[Hebrews 5:11 AMPC].** When a person has this problem, it is hard for others to explain things to them! The fault is not with the "subject" nor the "presenter," but with the "listener"! Prophet Isaiah wrote of such people, and Jesus applied it to many in His day in **[Matthew 13:13-15].** Many are like this because they are dull of heart and hearing, and as a result, they are prevented from:

1. *Understanding God's truth,*
2. *Turning from sin to God.*
3. *And hindered from being healed and saved by God!*

We do not want to be this type of listener or believer?

2. **THE SECOND KIND OF LISTENERS ACCORDING TO SCRIPTURE IS THOSE WITH "ITCHING EARS"**
[2nd Timothy 4:3-4 AMPC].

Such people listen only to that which is pleasing to them; so, they do not like the truth; they lack "sound doctrine" required in **[2nd Timothy 4:2 AMPC].**
Such people will find teachers and preachers they want that turn from the truth to fables: Many people today are afflicted with this "hearing" problem because of their itching ears!

3. THE THIRD KIND OF LISTENERS ACCORDING TO SCRIPTURE IS THOSE WHO HEAR WITH "A NOBLE AND GOOD HEART" [Luke 8:15]

The Bereans were listeners of this kind – **[Acts 17:11 NIV]** *"Now the Berean Jews were of more noble character than those in Thessalonica, for they received the message with great eagerness and examined the Scriptures every day to see if what Paul said was true."*
They were *"fair-minded,"* according to the **[NKJV],** thus willing to give Paul a fair hearing. That showed how they "received" [or listened to] the word: "with all readiness"; this is the kind of listener we all should be and thrive on being! ***But why is it so important to be this kind of listener?   There are several reasons: we shall learn about them in our next lesson.***

Memory Verse: [Hebrews 5:11] *"Of whom we have many things to say, which are hard to utter seeing ye are dull of hearing."*

December 13th

AFFLICTION

[Psalm 34:19] *"Many are the afflictions of the righteous: but the Lord delivereth him out of them all.*

Affliction is programmed difficulties and hardship. It is suffering, struggling, and enduring life when you should be enjoying life. It is a place of multiple frustrations. It is facing the storms of life defeated. When your life is flooded with troubles and even your money cannot help. Affliction is when you are bombarded with attacks from all angles like Job.

Affliction has no respect for anyone. It can come at any time, often suddenly and unexpectedly. Friends may abandon you, even trusted ones. Your level of education is irrelevant. Money and wealth cannot help. Your best bet is to invite God into the situation quickly. The Bible says, *do not put your trust in chariots, in princes or horses.*

Some afflictions are inherited. Examples are the descendants of Gehazi and Joab. It could be personal afflictions from evil covenants and curses, repercussions of unconfessed sin. You are afflicted when good things stay away from you and helpers stay away. You become over-ambitious, over suspicious, doing the right things at the wrong time, confusion and mental disorder, aggression towards others. You antagonize your divine helpers. *But I pray that every source of affliction in your life shall perish to ashes today in Jesus' Name. Amen!*

TESTIMONY TUESDAY

I FEEL I CAN OWN ANYTHING

My life has never been the same. Since I connected with you through Instagram in October 2019, I now feel I can own anything Good as written in God's Word. God owns the heavens and Earth and everything therein, and He is the one I believe in, so why not? **[Psalm 24:1].**

If you believe in the God of the Oracle, who owns everything, trust me, you will see and experience His miracles, signs, and wonders! I have indeed encountered the God of the Oracle through the Ministry of **Apostle Stevie Okauru.**

I have also learned that midnight prayers are the keys to opening spiritual gates to everything I need from God. Nothing leaves from Heaven until it is being released from the earth with midnight prayers! It works!

Praying is now no longer boring for me. It is now part of me. I thank God for anointing His servant Apostle Okauru through his ministrations and prophetic words; God is now re-aligning my life spiritually and bombarding me with all kinds of miraculous testimonies physically. I praise His Holy Name! Brother Jon Besot. Monrovia Liberia.

Prayer: *I key into this testimony, let me encounter Your Power in Jesus' Name. Amen!*

WEDNESDAY, December 15th

DEEP DIGGING: **LISTENING Part 3 of 7**
THE IMPORTANCE OF GOOD LISTENING

[**Mark 4:24**] *"Then He said to them, "Take heed what you hear. With the same measure you use, it will be measured to you; and to you who hear, more will be given."*

#1. ESSENTIAL TO BEING BLESSED: For those willing to listen correctly, there are beautiful things to learn [**Matthew 13:16-17**].   Many things that great people like David, Daniel, did not have the opportunity to learn: Things about beautiful blessings are now available in Christ! [**Ephesians 1:3**]. *Many miss out on these blessings because they do not listen carefully!*

#2. ESSENTIAL TO SAVING FAITH: God has ordained that we be saved through faith in Christ, and faith comes by hearing the gospel: [**Romans 1:16-17**]. Also, such faith comes through proclaiming the gospel, which often involves listening to a preacher. [**Romans 10:14; Romans 10:17**]. While one can certainly gain faith through reading God's Word, the fact remains that many are often dependent upon what they first hear proclaimed in preaching. [**John 20:30-31**]. Faith is often lacking because many are not good listeners, so they miss out on the evidence in God's Word, which produces faith! *Does your "listening" hinder the development of your faith?*

<h1 align="center">December 16th</h1>

THE LORD'S HAND

"For I was hungry, and you gave Me food; I was thirsty, and you gave Me drink; I was a stranger, and you took Me in." **[Matthew 25:35]**

During the Second World War, a church in Strasburg, Germany, was destroyed; but Christ's statue stood almost unharmed by the altar. Only the hands of the figure were missing. When the church was rebuilt, a famous sculptor offered to remake new hands for it, but the members decided to let it be as it was—without hands after considering the matter. "They said, *"Christ has no hands but our hands to do His work on earth."*
If we do not feed the hungry, give drink to the thirsty, entertain strangers, visit imprisoners, and clothe the naked, who will?" Christ depends on us to do the things He did while on earth. If the gospel we preach does not have a social application, it is not the Gospel of Christ if it will not work effectively.
Are you helping people? Are they taking beneficial advantage of your service in the vineyard? If so, give God Praise!
<u>Prayer:</u> *Lord Jesus, I ask this day that You use my hands for your glory. Make me conscious of the needs of those who hurt in the Name of Jesus Christ. Amen!*

December 17th

UNRIVALED FAITH!

[Hebrew 11:19] *"Accounting that God was able to raise him, even from the dead; from whence also he received him in a figure."*

An illustration of true faith is Charles Blondin's story, the French tightrope walker, whose fame came in September 1860, when he became the first person to cross a tightrope stretching 11,000 feet across the Niagara Falls several times: Each time with a different, daring feat. Once in a sack, on stilts, on a bicycle, in the dark and blindfolded. Then Blondin suddenly stopped and addressed his audience: *"Do you believe I can carry a person across in this wheelbarrow?"* The crowd yelled, "Yes! You are the greatest tightrope walker in the world. We believe!" "Okay," said Blondin, "Who wants to get into the wheelbarrow." No one did! This story illustrates a real-life picture of what faith is. The crowd watching the daring feats say they believed. But their actions proved otherwise.

Faith is the works of obedience. **[James 2:17]. [Hebrews 11:17-22]**, **[Romans 4:16-21]** examines what authenticates faith that Abraham exhibited. Like Abraham's, true faith always obeys God without doubt, which is the evidence to show that you believe and love Him. Obedience to His Word attracts innumerable and everlasting blessings. Saint! *Let your actions of faith speak the loudest henceforth in Jesus' Name.*

December 18th

WORD OF THE ORACLE

[**2nd Corinthians 4:7**] *"But we have this treasure in* **_earthen vessels_**, *that the excellence of the power may be of God and not of us."*

EARTHEN VESSELS [GREEK]: *"OSTRAKINOS SHEUOS"*

The Greek term for *'Earthen Vessels'* is ***"Ostrakinos Sheuos,"*** as used in the above text-verse and in [**2nd Timothy 2:20**]. Strong Concordance #3749 and 4632.

This Greek phrase means *"clay pots."* In ancient times it was a common practice to bury treasures inside clay jars.

Two recent biblical manuscripts: *The Chester Beatty Papyrus and some of the Dead Sea Scrolls,* reveal that these manuscripts were hidden away in clay jars for nearly two thousand years.

As these treasures were enclosed in earthen vessels, the indwelling Christ lives within our earthly bodies.

Prayer *Lord Jesus! Let Your Spirit dwell richly inside of me!*

ONE YEAR BIBLE PLAN: Micah 5-7/Rev. Chap. 8&9

SUNDAY SCHOOL
LISTENING Part 4 of 7

1. **ESSENTIAL TO BEARING FRUIT:** In the parable of the sower, the only kind of soil [heart] capable of bearing sustaining fruit is the listening heart. **[Luke 8:15].**
That is because bearing fruit comes from "understanding" God's grace! **[Colossians 1:6 TLB].**
And it is only by listening well can we "understand" God's grace and be motivated to bear fruit to His glory!

2. **ESSENTIAL TO PREVENTING APOSTASY:** There is a real danger of drifting by neglecting *"so great a salvation"* **[Hebrews 2:1-3].** The solution is to *"give more earnest heed to the things we have heard of the gospel"* because poor listening is often the first step to apostasy!

3. **ESSENTIAL TO AVOIDING REJECTION AND CONDEMNATION:** If we do not listen as we should, those who teach God's Word have a right to reject us: **[Matthew 10:14-15].** When we reject the Gospel, we judge ourselves unworthy of eternal life: **[Acts 13:44-49].** If we reject the gospel [perhaps because of poor listening], the men of Nineveh and the queen of the South will

condemn us at the judgment! **[Matthew 12:41-42].**

The men of Nineveh repented after hearing just one sermon from Jonah. ***Do we reject the gospel of Christ after being given many opportunities?***
The queen of the South went to great lengths to hear the wisdom of Solomon. ***Are we willing to go just a short distance to hear God's Word proclaimed?***
The rejection and condemnation are not limited to coming from individuals; it will come from God, too!
Hopefully, as we appreciate the beautiful opportunities to listen to God's Word and the importance of good listening, we can access all the blessings from listening to the gospel!
 But how then can we improve our ability to listen?
Just as speakers need to learn to speak to be understood, people need to learn to listen to understand!
We shall learn more in our next lesson.

ONE YEAR BIBLE PLAN: NAH 1-3/REV. CHAP.
10&11

BORN TO REIGN Part 1 of 2

[John 3:8] *"The wind bloweth where it listeth, and thou hearest the sound thereof, but canst not tell whence it cometh, and whither it goeth: so is every one that is born of the Spirit."*

What Does it Mean to Be "Born"? To be "born" is a spiritual rebirth. **[Ephesians 2:13-18].** It means to be born of the Spirit of God. **[John 3:8].** It means to become the temple of Father, Son, and the Holy Spirit. It means to become a member of God's family.

It is to reign is to rule. **[Ephesians 1:17-23, Genesis 37:8].** Jesus reigns forever as King of Kings and Lord of Lords. **[Exodus 15:18].** As born-again Christians are children of God, we are joint heirs with Christ of all that our Father possesses. He owns everything. We are complete in Him and seated with Christ in Heavenly places. Therefore, we are reigning with Him. **[Colossians 2:10, Revelation 5:9-14, Ephesians 2:6].**

To reign means that in Christ, we are prophets, priests, and kings. **[Revelation 5:10].** It means that we are Christ's ambassadors. **[2nd Corinthians 5:20].** We rule on earth in His stead. We become an extension of God's hands-on earth. **[Mark 16:17-18].**

TESTIMONY TUESDAY

Praise Jesus! I want to give thanks, Praise, Glory, and honor to our Lord and Savior, Jesus Christ.

I have a lot to share, but I would only say this: I was Praying for my friend and cousin who were sick, my cousin is in the United Kingdom, and she has been ill for a long time. One morning on the prayer conference of Apostle Okauru, the Oracle of God, he mentioned her case specifically and declared that God had healed her. Two days later, she was discharged from ICU. She is now wholly whole and back to work. Glory to God!

My friend had fibroid, and she was scheduled for surgery, but a week to the day of the operation on the prayer conference line, Apostle Okauru declares that there is somebody here the fibroid that needs an operation, is melting away now by the fire of God in the Name of Jesus Christ.

That night my friend, my roommate, passed out the fibroid in the toilet, and thus she needed no surgery, and there is no more fibroid in her system. I give God all glory and honor. Merilyn Dean. Dublin, Ireland.

Are you sick? As the Oracle of God, I decree and declare in the Name of our Lord and Savior Jesus Christ, receive your healing by the healing fire of God in Jesus' Mighty Name. Amen!

WEDNESDAY, December 22nd

DEEP DIGGING: **LISTENING Part 5 of 7**
STEPS TO BETTER LISTENING

#1. MAKE LISTENING AN ACT OF WORSHIP: How you listen to God's Word being read, taught, and preached is as much an indication of your devotion to God as to how you pray, praise, and worship Him. So, when you have opportunities to listen, do it with "a worshipful attitude."

Think of how you would listen if some great persons spoke; imagine your rapt attention if you heard some famous person speaking. ***Does not God's Word deserve as much attention?***

#2. LISTEN FROM FIRST TO LAST: That is paying attention through and through. No one understands a novel by merely reading a sentence here and there. So, it is with listening to God's Word. Sentences, phrases, clauses, words can only be understood considering the context in which they are presented.

Speakers usually follow specific rules to be understood. *A] They introduce the subject. B] Present main points with supporting arguments. C] And conclude with a summary:*

So, should a good listener; listen to ALL the parts of a statement to utterly understand.

The grace to be a better listener receive it now in the Name of Jesus Christ. Amen!

December 23rd

BORN TO REIGN Part 2 of 2

Reigning means that we are lions after the order of the Lion of Judah. **[Revelation 5:5, Proverbs 28:1].**

We are victors and not victims. We are delivered from our enemies who are now under our feet just like they are under Jesus' feet. **[1st Corinthians 15:25, Luke 1:74, Ephesians 1:22, Psalm 8:4-8].**

Reigning portrays being the head and not the tail, being above and not beneath. **[Deuteronomy 28:13, Colossians 1:18].** It means occupying until Jesus comes back. **[Luke 19:13].**

Reigning means that we have authority through God's Word, the Blood of Jesus, the Name of Jesus Christ, the fire of the Holy Ghost fire, and other weapons that are available to us as Christians.

It is having dominion over sin, self, flesh, circumstances, demon, and Satan. **[Genesis 1:26-28, Genesis 27:40, Isaiah 43:2, Luke 10:18-19].** Reigning portrays a person of honor, glory, and power. It involves doing the "greater works than Jesus did" because Jesus has delegated that assignment and the power to do it to us. **[John 14:12].**

Hindrances to Ruling and Reigning

    I. Ignorance **[Hosea 4:6]**

    II. Sin **[Roman 6:12, 2nd Timothy 2:19]**

    III. Disobedience **[2nd Corinthians 10:6]**

    IV. Prayerlessness **[1st Thessalonians 5:17]**

    V. Fear **[Joshua 1:9]**

VI. Failure to use God-given authority and weapons. **[Luke 10:19]**

VII. Captivity **[2ⁿᵈ Timothy 2:26]**

VIII. The satanic onslaught from powers such as household wickedness **[Genesis 37:8, Matthew 10:36]**

IX. Curses, covenants, and bad foundation **[Psalm 11:3]**

X. Unwilling to suffer for Christ. **[2ⁿᵈ Timothy 2:11-12].**

XI. Laziness **[Proverb 12:24, Proverbs 24:30]**

Way Out

a) Get born again. **[John 3:3-7]**

b) Stay away from sin. **[Proverbs 28:13]**

c) Be thoroughly prayed up and fasted up. **[Matthew 17:21]**

d) Know your rights and heritage as a child of God. **[Galatians 4:1]**

e) Clean up your foundation and ensure your deliverance is complete. **[Psalm 11:3; Obadiah 17]**

December 24th

[2nd king 2:15] *"...At Jericho saw him, they said the spirit of Elijah rest on Elisha, and they came to meet him, and they bowed down to him."*

MOCKERS SHALL BOW!

The Spirit of God is going to come upon you today, and a new anointing will be operational in your life in Jesus' Name.

In **[2nd Kings 2:1-15],** the other sons of the prophet mocked the diligence of Elisha. But when a double portion of Elijah's spirit came upon Elisha and he smite River Jordan, he instantly gained the reverence of all the prophets in Israel.

Have mockers and scorners mocked you? Has your Christian faith been ridiculed? Have you been discriminated against and humiliated for your faith in Christ Jesus? Hold on to the plow, for the anointing that breaks the yoke is coming upon you now! *I decree every jester in your life, will be uprooted this day in Jesus' Name. Amen!*

In **[Mark 10:46-52],** those who were telling Bartimeus to shut up were the same people that Jesus sent to get him, and when they saw him with brand new eyes, they celebrated him. *I declare; you will be honored. I prophesy those who are mocking you now will come and celebrate with you!*

Prayer: *I decree my mockers must bow to me!*

<h1 align="center">December 25th</h1>

WORD OF THE ORACLE

[2nd Corinthians 5:21] *"For He made Him who knew no sin to be sin for us, that we might become the* <u>***righteousness of God***</u> *in Him."*

RIGHTEOUSNESS OF GOD [GREEK]: *"DIKAIOSUNE THEO."*

The Greek term for *'Righteousness of God'* is *"Dikaiosune Theo"* as used in the above text-verse and in **[Romans 1:17, Romans 3:21-22 and Romans 10:3].** Strong's Concordance #1343 and #2316. The righteousness of God is the righteousness that comes from God. It is God's way of making a sinner right, or just, before Him. It is the righteousness valid before God, which a man may possess through faith. This righteousness is the first and the last need of any sinful person.

The word righteousness in Paul's letter to the Romans carries a double sense and may be both legal and moral. In other words, the word refers to the legal action God takes in declaring believers righteous, but it also refers to perfect righteousness, a characteristic that can only be attributed to God Himself in Scripture. And this is the highest standard; a standard no one's effort can achieve or attian. So, God must act to bring His people into the right relationship with Himself.

Fourth Sunday in December

SUNDAY SCHOOL: **BETTER LISTENING Part 6 of 7**

1. **LOOK AT THE SPEAKER:** This greatly aids your concentration: Looking elsewhere makes it easy for your mind to wander. Closing your eyes makes it easy for you to nod off! All these require self-discipline, but it is conducive to developing a longer attention span: *Try it and see if it does not make a difference in your listening skill set!*

2. **READ ALONG IN YOUR BIBLE:** You remember more of what you both see and hear over what you simply hear, which is why visual aids are often used in sermons. But the most significant visual assistance is your own Bible! Your knowledge of the Scriptures can be significantly improved by doing this, though it is hard at first to keep up with. But if you persevere, it will soon become more comfortable. *We encourage our children to do this; let us do the same?*

3. **LISTEN WITH FAITH:** Listen with a willingness to accept and believe God's Word. **[Hebrews 4:1-2]**. Those who died in the wilderness did not listen with a heart of faith! *If we do not listen "with faith," the same happens to us; that is, we fall short of our heavenly rest!*

4. **LISTEN WITH A MIND TO ACT:** We must not be like the people in Ezekiel's day? **[Ezekiel 33:30-32]**. They loved to hear him, but for the wrong reason. The hearing must be followed by doing; for it to be profitable **[James 1:22-25]**.

EVIL COUNSEL CANCELED

".... And David said, O LORD, I pray thee, turn the counsel of Ahithophel into foolishness". **[2nd Samuel 15:31]**

Ahithophel was a sage man. He was a master strategist. According to scriptures, his counsel was divine. But in one single prayer, David turned him to a foolish man **[2nd Samuel 15:31]** because he dared to take sides against a man who was on God's side. *The Lord shall turn every Ahithophel of your life to fools in the Name of Jesus Christ!* **[2nd Samuel 17:23].** Ahithophel's defection was very painful to David because the man was an insider in David's cabinet.

Many are in trouble because an insider has joined forces with their enemies. Some people are unable to conceive and bear children because an insider is monitoring their conceptions. Some are unable to breakthrough because someone they trust so much is divulging vital information to their enemies. Some are limited because a family member is invoking the power of curses over their lives.

If you are in any category, fear not, for the Lord has remembered you today. *So, I prophesy, every evil counsel against you is turned to foolishness. Like Ahithophel counsel, those evil messengers shall have their information rejected in Jesus' Name. Amen!*

TESTIMONY TUESDAY

Praise the Lord! Since I got introduced to your prayer conference over a year ago, and I can say the Lord has done a lot for me in the first ninety days of this year than in the last nine years of my life.

I got a fantastic breakthrough after I participated in the annual thirty days fasting and praying from January 5th to February 3rd, 2021. All the negativity and disappointments in my life have been reversed to God's glory.

Now great doors are opening because of the $120.00 "No Carryover Crossover Seed" that I sowed during the fasting and praying as Apostle Stevie Okauru admonished us to sow. Glory to God.

I was about to miss out on something God has for me, but God has come through for me on time. The Lord is also recovering and restoring many divine connections I lost.

I know I will have my best year yet in life this year, in the Name of Jesus Christ. Amen!

Ann-Janet Moses, Charlotte NC

ONE YEAR BIBLE PLAN: ZECH. 11-12/REV20:1-15

DEEP DIGGING: **LISTENING Part 7 of 7**
BENEFIT OF BETTER LISTENING

How important, then, is listening? When it comes to listening to God, it is essential! **[Isaiah 55:2-3]**. Proper listening is crucial for the good of our soul!

Is there ever a time when GOD does not listen? Yes, when our sins stand between God and us **[Isaiah 59:1-2]** But we can take care of that problem by receiving God's Mercy **[Isaiah 55:6-7]**

Today, that mercy is offered through Jesus Christ, God's Son. And as God said: *"This is My Beloved Son. Hear Him!"* **[Luke 9:35]**

Have you heeded Him by obeying His word?
Or does the following cry of Jesus apply to you...?
"But why do you call Me 'Lord, Lord,' and do not do the things which I say?" **[Luke 6:46]**

<h1 style="text-align:center">December 30th</h1>

COMPLETE IN CHRIST

"Blessed be the God and Father of our Lord Jesus Christ, who has blessed us with every spiritual blessing in the heavenly places in Christ." **[Ephesians 1:3]**

In **[Ephesians 1:3-14]**, we see the manifestation of the Trinity – God the Father, the Son, and the Holy Spirit – **[verse 3, verse 13]** showing the believer's position in Christ. God has chosen us in Christ and adopted us into His family through Jesus. In Christ, we have redemption and the forgiveness of sins, making God's grace abound towards us in all wisdom and prudence. Therefore, we are sealed with Holy Spirit as a guarantee that He is in us, with us, and for us.

The implications of these spiritual blessings include thanksgiving and duty. In **[verse 3]**, we give thanks: *"Blessed be the God and Father of our Lord Jesus Christ, who hath blessed us with all spiritual blessings in heavenly places in Christ."* The blessings are all-inclusive; we should give Him thanks for that. Again, the blessings imply to us the duty of *"...walking worthy..."* of the position in Christ **[Ephesians 4:1]. We** are complete in Him.

<u>Prayer:</u> *Lord, help me see my position in Christ.*

December 31st

[Psalm 65:11 AKJV] *"You crown the year with your goodness, and your paths drop fatness."*

1. *Thank You, Lord, for crowning my year with goodness!*

2. *Thank You for pouring down abundance on my loved ones.* **[Job 36:28].**

3. *The Lord has made me lie down in green pastures and leads me beside still waters.* **[Psalm 23:2].**

4. *Lord, thank You for satisfying us with good things.* **[Psalm 104:28].**

5. *Father Lord, thank You for granting us peace to our borders and satisfies us with the finest of wheat.* **[Psalm 147:14].**

6. *God will crown my New Year with His goodness and drop fatness on my paths.* **[Psalm 65:11].**

7. *I decree God will grant me abundance, crown me with glory, and crown the New Year with financial plenty in Jesus' Name. Amen! Glory to God!*

8. *Let the Word of God that is quick, powerful, and sharper than any two-edged sword; pierces through every negative thought or speech I have ever made and tear them down in Jesus' Name. Amen!*

9. *I trust in the Lord, and I lean not on my understanding.*

10. *Lord fill my heart with Your Words of faith; I receive and speak Your Words of faith in Jesus' Name. Amen!*

happy sunday